INDIAN DRAWING

An exhibition chosen by Howard Hodgkin
Introduction by Terence McInerney

Arts Council of Great Britain 1983

LENDERS

UK

Cambridge, Fitzwilliam Museum
London, British Library, India Office Library and Records
London, Sven Gahlin
London, Lisbet Holmes
London, Victoria & Albert Museum
Norwich, University of East Anglia, The Robert and Lisa Sainsbury Collection
Private collections

AUSTRALIA

Melbourne, National Gallery of Victoria

USA

Dr. Alvin O. Bellak
The Catherine and Ralph Benkaim Collection
Private collections

An Arts Council touring exhibition

Hayward Gallery, London 10 February–17 April 1983
Wolverhampton Art Gallery 23 April–21 May 1983
Herbert Art Gallery, Coventry 4 June–10 July 1983
Bolton Museum and Art Gallery 16 July–20 August 1983
Graves Art Gallery, Sheffield 27 August–2 October 1983

ACKNOWLEDGEMENT

In 1982 the Festival of India heightened our appreciation of all forms of Indian art and the Arts Council was particularly pleased when Howard Hodgkin, who has long been keenly interested in Indian art, accepted an invitation to select an exhibition of Indian drawings. He has developed his own view of the art of Indian drawing in his introduction to the exhibition.

We are further indebted to Howard Hodgkin for the preparation of the catalogue notes. We would also like to thank Terence McInerney, who has advised Mr. Hodgkin, and contributed an informative introductory essay on the technique of Indian drawing, and some of the catalogue notes.

Thanks are also due to Professor Cary Welch, Mr. Robert Skelton, Professor Milo Beach and Mr. Andrew Topsfield for their help in the preparation of the exhibition.

Finally, the Arts Council wishes to thank all the lenders, both public institutions and private collectors, many of whom wish to remain anonymous.

JOANNA DREW
Director of Art

INTRODUCTION TO THE EXHIBITION

This exhibition was arranged by an artist. A lot of nonsense has been written about the 'Artist's Eye' – it's certainly not superior but possibly a bit different. But anyway how would I know? As an artist I can choose what I like, a privilege for which I am grateful but one not available to the scholar or art historian.

My love for Indian drawing is something I want to share with other people. But it is based on feeling rather than knowledge, and so this exhibition is neither comprehensive nor historical. Few of these drawings come from museums because they don't have many. Most are from private collections, many from my own.

When I first became interested in Indian drawings and began to collect them I succumbed to the easy temptation of equating them with great European drawings of a kind I would never be able to possess. This one reminded me of an Ingres, that one was like a Rembrandt. The only advantage of these rather silly comparisons was to make me realise how unlike European works Indian drawings actually are. Tentatively at first, I began to see them as great drawings in their own right, executed in a language entirely their own.

But there were other attractions. They reminded me of India in a manner that was both intense and impersonal. The foreignness of the subject matter, and at the same time its curious familiarity, were moving in a detached sort of way. And my ignorance of style and iconography enabled me to enjoy these beautiful drawings without needing to worry about what they actually were. The subject matter retained its innocent enchantments: a ruler visiting a holy man in a garden, a prince hunting lions, an exquisite portrait of an animal. But inevitably as I learned more about them by making comparisons between one drawing and another, the rot set in, and I started making value judgements. From then on, I began to have endless conversations with friends on this fascinating subject. With Professor Cary Welch of Harvard, whom I first met many years ago when I took some drawings to the Indian Section of the Victoria and Albert Museum for an opinion. He was typically forthright in his reactions. Not only has he a celestial gift of the gab when talking about Indian art, he is also a world authority on the subject; and his encouragement and enthusiasm have meant much to me over the years. Also with Robert Skelton, now Keeper of the Indian Section, who was also present on the same occasion and who has remained a constant and articulate prisoner's friend. (All collectors are prisoners.) And finally with Terence McInerney who has written the introduction to this catalogue, and who better late than never, opened my eyes to Mughal art.

Drawing is the most naked of the visual arts. Sometimes we can feel an almost physical contact with the artist and share in the workings of his mind and imagination. We learn to recognise and identify with certain marks on paper, traces of pencil and gouache, the speed of execution and the possibilities of various media, the genuine searches and intentional errors. The human element is paramount, so we feel we know when we are being told lies by the draftsman.

But our familiarity with these things can act as a barrier when we start looking at Indian drawings because at first they look so physically alike. For example, the emphasis on artistic personality, the self-revelation of a single human being, that is so familiar in Western art is not often found in Indian art. And it is all too easy to equate the loose and calligraphic with an individual hand. Nor do we find human emotion expressed in any direct way. Perhaps the nearest we get to it in this exhibition is in the affecting, almost life-size drawing of two girls with faces touching (no. 11), or, with a far more generalised reticence, in the portraits (nos. 2, 3 and 7). However, pantheistic feelings about nature abound, not only in images of animals such as the ubiquitous elephants, but also in the mysterious visual life given to the portrayal of plants and trees.

The Indian landscape, in so far as one can generalise at all is mostly quite empty and very dusty with a general tone and colour of beige and cream not unlike the tint of much of the paper that is used for these drawings. The sun and the light that comes from it are so bright and hard that the edges of everything, whether leaf, stone, hill, building, animal or man, are very sharp. Even morning and evening pass in a flash. Shadows are cutouts. The light is so bright that the modelling of surfaces is quite shallow. The scale is also different from what one is used to. The even illumination negates distance, so that the enormity of space is quite visible and everything looks and feels small.

Apart from the technicalities of drawing with brush and ink, there may be another reason for the almost totally linear foundation of Indian drawings. In an Indian situation, a tree is a tree. If it is depicted surrounded by blank paper, it is none the less representational. The one-to-one relationship between a drawn shape and its counterpart in nature is both finite and literal. There are no saving clauses, no sudden descents into mysterious calligraphy or romantic vagueness, no hopeful journeys into the unknown. All is clear and, if not exact, at least concrete.

The delicately coloured, unfinished landscape (reproduced on the cover of the catalogue) is of an astonishing fidelity to anyone who has been to Kotah. But it lacks the enclosing envelope of light that we would expect to find in Western art. In this drawing, the trees cast no shadows. Likewise when we look at the modelling on an elephant's belly or, more rarely, on a man's face, it doesn't really reveal an effect of light. Rather like braille, it demonstrates the tactile quality of the form. Volume is more often implied than described. Indian draftsmen must surely be among the absolute masters of enclosing a weighty form between two simple lines, leaving the spectator to fill in what lies between.

Among the different subjects represented in this exhibition such as the durbar, tiger hunts, human and animal portraits, etc., elephants predominate. This is partly because I have a particular love of drawings of elephants. But there is also a better reason: good Indian drawings of elephants are more frequently encountered than drawings of any other subject. Human beings in particular are not nearly as elaborately or as enthusiastically depicted.

Perhaps the shifting volume and surface, the loose skin and the obvious structure inside it, the colossal weight which can defy gravity with a leap in the air and then sink to the ground in a heap like a mountain, were to the Indian artist what the changing forms and moods of the naked human body are supposed to have been to the Post-Renaissance European artist.

Howard Hodgkin

INDIAN DRAWING

Indian draughtsmen were virtuosi of the brush. They used charcoal on occasion, for underdrawing or preliminary ideas; and the amateur or village artist might use a reed pen. But the tradition as a high art, the drawings that comprise the present exhibition, were made with a brush. Indeed with only one exception (no. 28), all of the works included here are brush drawings on paper. And what an enormous range of line and feeling they contain! A draughtsman like Basawan, the sixteenth-century Mughal master, had a command of the brush, in terms of the variety and texture of his line, that is really only rivalled by the Chinese. His drawings, whether slight sketches, finished preparatory studies (no. 50), or autonomous works of art (nos. 1, 52), often look like chalk or pen drawings; and his hatching or stippling suggests the engraved line. Yet Basawan achieved all of his incomparable effects with a brush alone.

A master of his distinction had an enormous number and variety of brushes with which to work. They were made from the finest materials, from the hairs of kittens or baby squirrels; and they varied in thickness and contour in the extreme. The finest brushes were virtually invisible: they were set with two or three hairs.

Similarly Indian paper varied greatly in texture, thickness and finish. It was handmade from cloth fibres, and several sheets were glued together to form the drawing base or support. The combination of papers employed, the quality and thickness of the constituent layers, allowed for fine tuning in adjusting the porous or resistant properties of the resulting drawing support. When desired, a particularly hard, gem-like surface was achieved by burnishing – polishing many laminations of fine-grained paper with an agate tool. The paper supports for the most detailed or highly finished drawings are prepared in this way (no. 17). Conversely, a rough, preliminary drawing for the artist's use alone is often made on one or two laminations of a particularly large-fibre, resilient paper that is wonderfully absorbent (no. 29). It welcomes rapid thought.

The distinction between an Indian painting and an Indian drawing is hardly extreme. The technique and materials used for each are more or less the same. Indian paintings, or 'miniatures' as they are often rather inaccurately called, are works on paper. Opaque watercolour is applied with a brush, following the plan established by a preliminary underdrawing. The painter's actual gestures are essentially graphic. His colour is applied in flat washes which are transparent or opaque, depending on the number of layers employed. Tints are never broken or scumbled as they are in European watercolours. Any significant lines that have been lost or concealed are then redrawn, in colour, on the finished work.

Many Indian drawings are really tinted sketches, some 'drawings' are in fact unfinished paintings (no. 35), while other works are neither paintings nor drawings, but a conscious blend of the two. These stylish hybrids are one of the most attractive, yet underrated, achievements of Indian art. (See nos. 10, 15, 23, 24, 32, 34, 41, 43, 44). Since the fine points and distinctions are endless, we offer for the sake of simplicity the following definitions: an Indian painting is a work that is fully coloured; an Indian drawing is a work where there are significant areas of paper left bare. Indian paintings conceal the very process that Indian drawings enshrine.

This process was by no means haphazard. The Indian artist was trained in a highly conceptual way. He did not begin his training by drawing from nature. Rather, he was set the task of repeating certain signs and symbols that had been codified for youthful instruction over the years. He was also trained in the proper language of the arabesque –

those abstractions of the energies and shapes of leaves and flowers – and in the other cursive, decorative motifs. The emphasis was on dexterity, rather than personal vision. He moved from abstraction to representation only as he acquired skill and facility as a technician.

These foundations in abstract theory give the Indian line its incomparably taut, resilient quality, which only the modern forgery belies. Indian drawings lack the variety and material seductions of European graphic works. There are no Indian drawings on parchment or coloured papers. There are no Indian studies in silverpoint or pencil, nor works in coloured chalks or pastel. The Indian artist was not interested in effects of light and dark, in atmosphere and tonal contrast, in the limitless space and transient light that preoccupied his Western colleagues. A Tiepolo sketchbook would have been poorly received in Delhi.

But the deceptive simplicity of technique and material did not hamper their emotional range. The Indian artist approached his subject with relentless intensity, with the desire to fix its essential appearance, for all time. He might play with abstraction, or risk expressive distortions of form. There was leeway in the representation, but the 'language' itself was fixed. Despite the bewildering array of styles, the Indian graphic tradition is essentially an art of contour drawing. The outline is never broken. And this principle, and perhaps only this principle, reigned supreme.

The Mughal dynasty, founded by Babur in 1526, established the drawing tradition that we are describing here. The earlier, pre-Mughal tradition of Indian painting had ossified into an art of repetitive and stereotyped compositions. The style was conceptual, two-dimensional, perfunctory in line and restricted in colour. It is perhaps no overstatement to call this earlier style 'medieval'. Indeed, if any drawings had survived from this period (and they have not, as far as one knows), they would have looked much like the drawings found in European pattern books, dating from the late Middle Ages, which have survived. One can make this deduction from the fairly large number of Indian paintings dating from the fifteenth century and earlier which still exist. These conceal little of the underdrawing that defines their overall structure. The lines are carefully wrought, defining inflexible contours and avoiding any suggestion of internal definition, or the rendering of form through hatching. In this world, the nature and purpose of drawings were strictly utilitarian.

Drawing emerged as an autonomous activity under Mughal patronage. Although Babur established the dynasty, it was really Akbar (r. 1556–1605), the third and most gifted ruler of the line, who inspired the decisive break with the past. The duty of an artist, in his view, was to sketch 'everything that has life'. The ramifications of this radical reappraisal of artistic purpose – the urge for a more direct and responsive observation of nature – were wide-ranging. A whole repertoire of new subjects – realistic portraiture and vivid scenes of daily life, natural history and scientific studies, landscape and urban views – were first introduced during Akbar's reign.

For the Akbari artist, drawing bridged the gap between the initial idea and the finished work. The complexity and ambition of their paintings required elaborate preparation in drawing. It is most unfortunate that so few drawings from this period, and from that of Akbar's successors, Jahangir (r. 1605–27) and Shah Jahan (r. 1627–58), have survived. Originally Mughal drawings of the classic period must have numbered in the tens of thousands. Yet from the few that have survived one can see that Mughal court artists used drawings in a way that would have been immediately familiar to a Renaissance artist, at least in terms of the inherent working processes involved.

Mughal artists sketched from life, making portrait (nos. 2, 3) or animal studies, or noting genre scenes encountered in daily life. These sketches might or might not reappear at a later date as the basis for a finished motif. These finished individual motifs were elaborated in many compositional or figural group studies of a preparatory nature (no. 49). They were harmonized in a highly detailed and finished drawing – a 'contract' drawing, so to speak – that served as the basis for the painted work (no. 39). The various stages in the evolution of the idea could be abbreviated somewhat, and incorporated on the same sheet, by 'correcting' lines in a different colour, or tone of ink, or by covering an original line with a whitener and redrawing. Once the elaborate structure of the finished work had been set down, the essential outlines of the 'contract' drawing were redrawn in simplified form on a sheet of paper that had been prepared for paint (no. 37). It was only now, after this final work had been sketched in as an underdrawing, that the actual act of painting commenced.

Not all Mughal drawings are preparatory studies or sketches from life. Indeed some of the most attractive Mughal drawings were made as autonomous works of art. These are always highly finished and minutely detailed; and they are almost always heightened with colour, or with the thin tan washes known as *nim kalam* (nos. 1, 52). These drawings are so polished they compare in technique and finish to actual paintings. Indeed they exist in lieu of paintings, but have the same aesthetic value.

For as long as the Mughal empire lasted, i.e. until 1857, the imperial court maintained a sophisticated drawing tradition, and a secular, humanistic approach, which constituted the high, metropolitan style for most of India. As its influence began to reach the feudal courts in outlying areas, a comparable sophistication of method and purpose began to take root elsewhere. Perhaps the most prolific and creative centre of drawing beyond the Mughal orbit was centred at Kotah, in Hindu Rajasthan. Indeed drawings from this provincial court rival Mughal drawings in range and variety. Yet while they are remarkably bold and expressive in a way a Mughal drawing would never be, Kotah drawings, in terms of process and purpose, are Mughal-inspired. Kotah drawings like Mughal drawings are primarily records of artistic and creative activities. When taken as a whole, they record a work in progress. When viewed individually, they record separate phases of an on-going process, the evolution of an idea from the initial sketch (no. 29), through the intermediary studies (no. 26), to the finalised work, the finished model for transfer (no. 31).

The Mughal influence was also felt as a positive force at other provincial centres. The small courts of Sawar, in Rajasthan (nos. 32, 33, 42, 46), and Chamba, in the Pubjab Hills (nos. 41, 44), developed a boldly abbreviated, highly expressive version of the Mughal sense of drawing that is most original. In fact the provincial, or Rajput, styles of Indian drawing are distinctive and varied. There were important centres at Udaipur, in Mewar (nos. 10, 34), and at Guler (no. 14) and Kishangarh (no. 13) as well. Yet for the purpose of generalisation it is safe to say that drawing reached its peak at various centres whenever it was pursued as an autonomous activity, as a flexible vehicle for artistic thought. It reached its nadir whenever it became subservient to the folkloric approach. The vast majority of Indian drawings are really a debased variety of folk art.

There are different things here.

TERENCE MCINERNEY

CATALOGUE

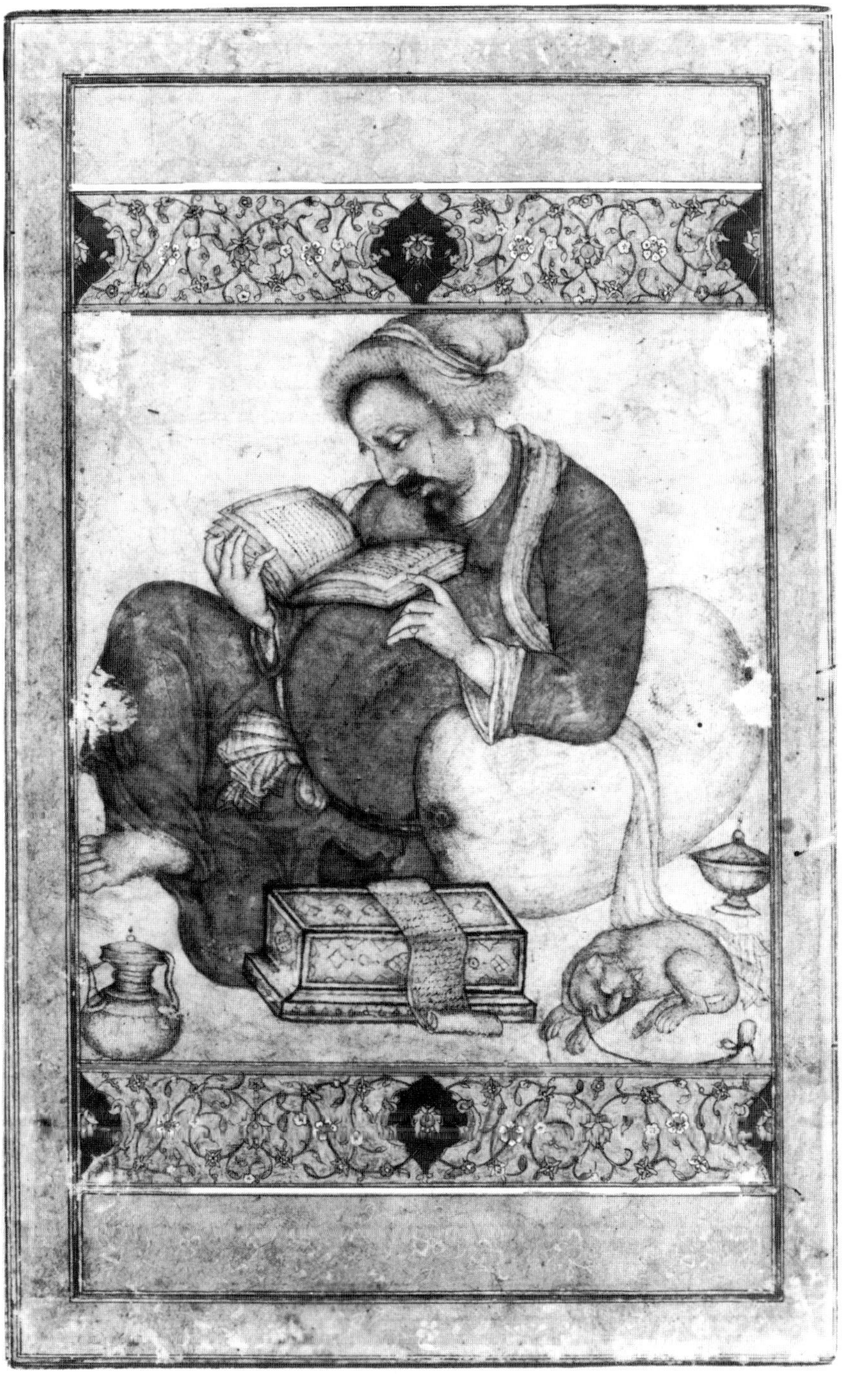

1 A learned man
Mughal, *c* 1575–80, attributed to Basawan
Black line with colour washes on paper 187 × 136 mm
Literature: S. C. Welch, 1976, no. 7
Private collection

This drawing by Basawan, one of the greatest and most sensitive of early Mughal painters (see nos. 50, 52), was part of an album assembled in 1611/12 for the Shah Jahan when still a Prince. On the back of the folio there is a long inscription in his hand. HH

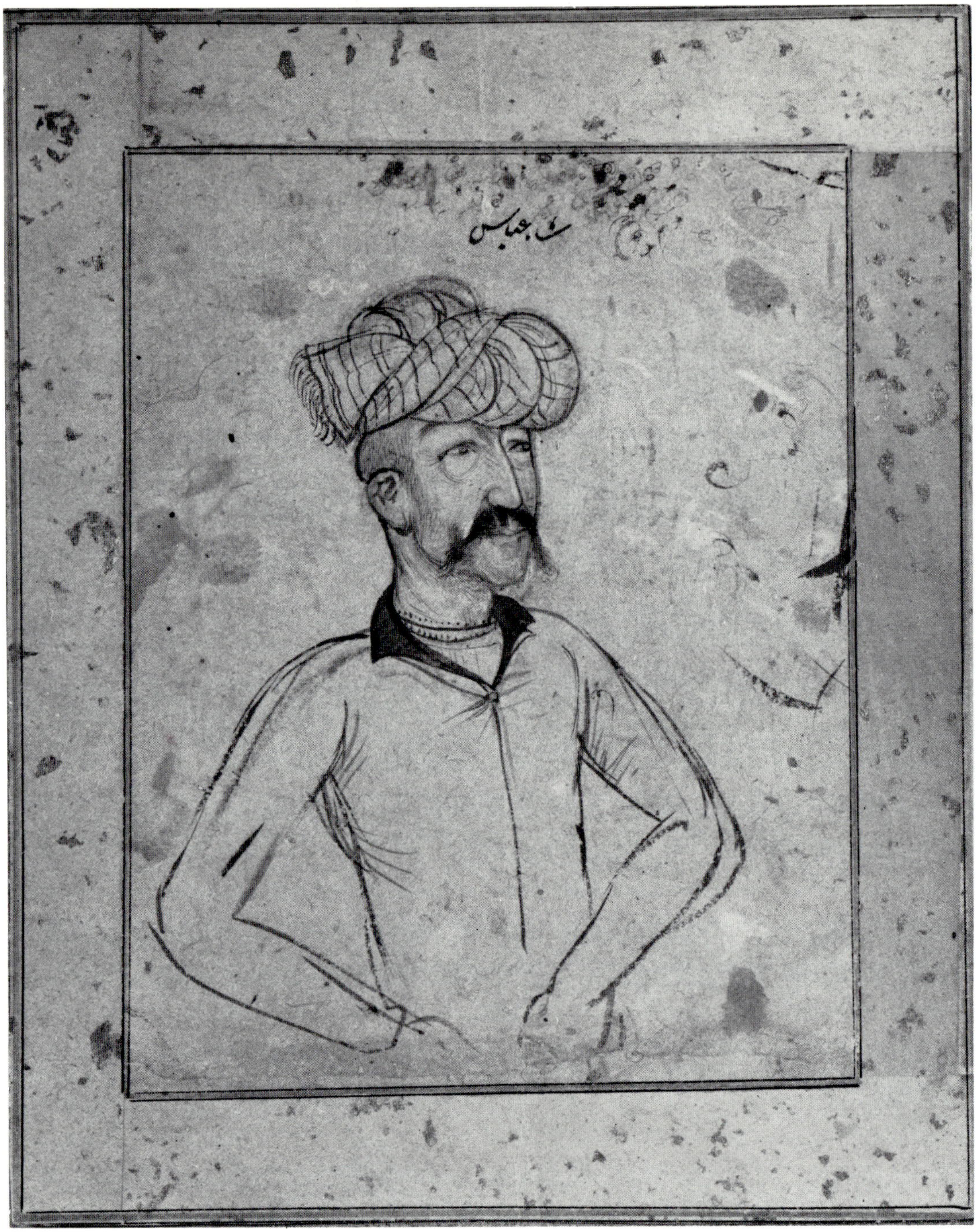

2 Shah Abbas I of Iran

Attributed to Bishan Das
Mughal, *c* 1615
Drawing in brush and black ink, heightened with white and colour, on paper. Pasted on a Kishangarh mount with gold-speckled borders 149 × 117 mm
Inscribed in Persian: *Shah Abbas*
Literature: M. C. Beach, 1978, pp. 107–111
Private collection

This sketch of one of Persia's greatest kings, Shah Abbas I (r. 1587–1629), was drawn from life by the renowned Mughal portrait painter Bishan Das (fl. 1590–1640). It would have been made after the year 1613 when Bishan Das was chosen to accompany the splendid embassy sent by Jahangir to impress and intimidate his 'royal brother' Shah Abbas. The pertinent details are found in Jahangir's memoirs, the *Tuzuk-i-Jahangiri*:

> 'At the time when I sent Khan Alam (as ambassador) to Persia, I had sent with him a painter of the name of Bishan Das, who was unequalled in his age for taking likenesses, to take the portraits of the Shah and the chief men of his State, and bring them. He had drawn the likenesses of most of them, and especially had taken that of my brother the Shah exceedingly well, so that when I showed it to any of his servants, they said it was exceedingly well done.' (Volume II, pp. 116–117)

Another version of this drawing is found in the Barberini Album in the Vatican Library. (See O. Kurz, 1977, pl. 7) TM

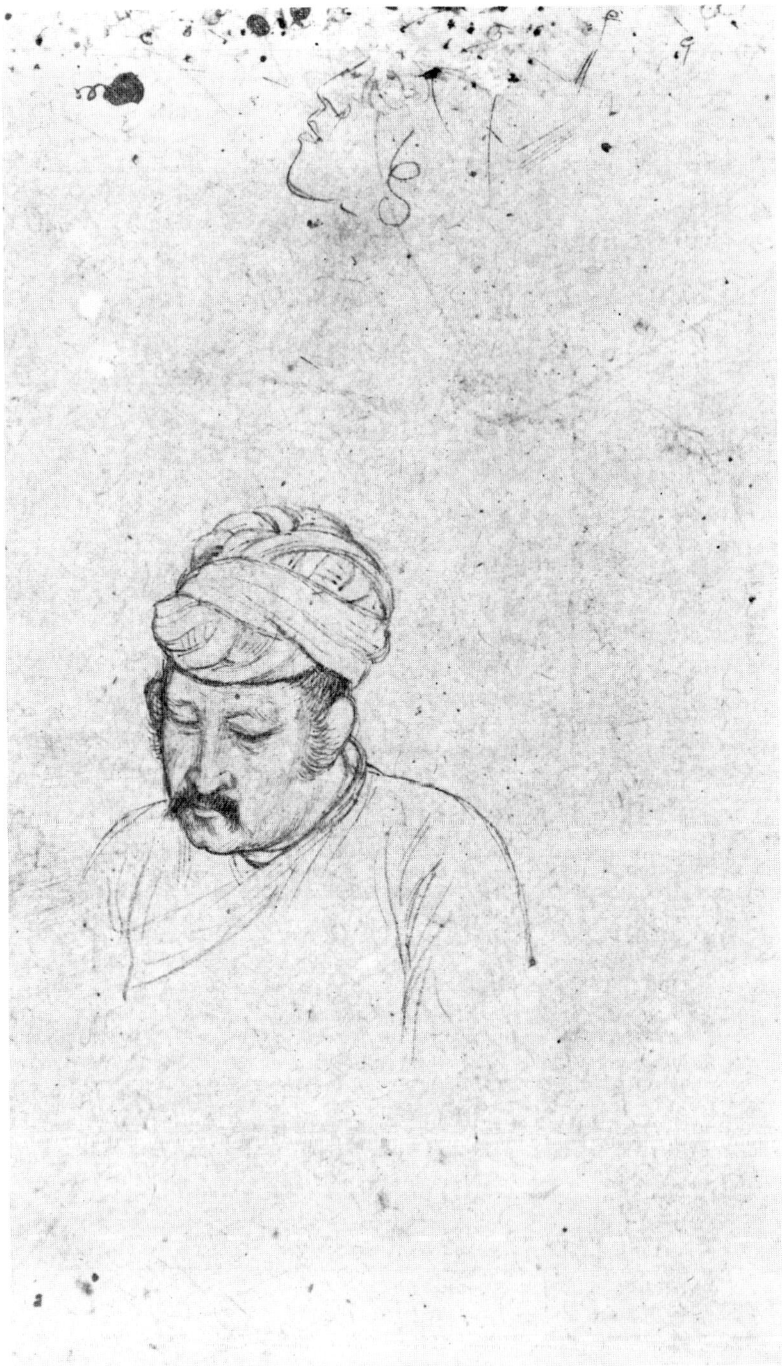

3 Portrait of Akbar (?)

Mughal, perhaps early seventeenth century
Drawing on paper with other sketches of a medallion and a girl's face; mounted with border of grey paper 133 × 130 mm; page 224 × 160 mm
Inscribed on reverse: *Akbar*; in Persian characters: *Akbar badshah* ('*the Emperor Akbar*'); numbered I
Literature: T. Falk and M. Archer, 1981, p. 114
British Library, India Office Library and Records

Though catalogued as being of later date, this drawing must surely have been done from life (see no. 2). HH

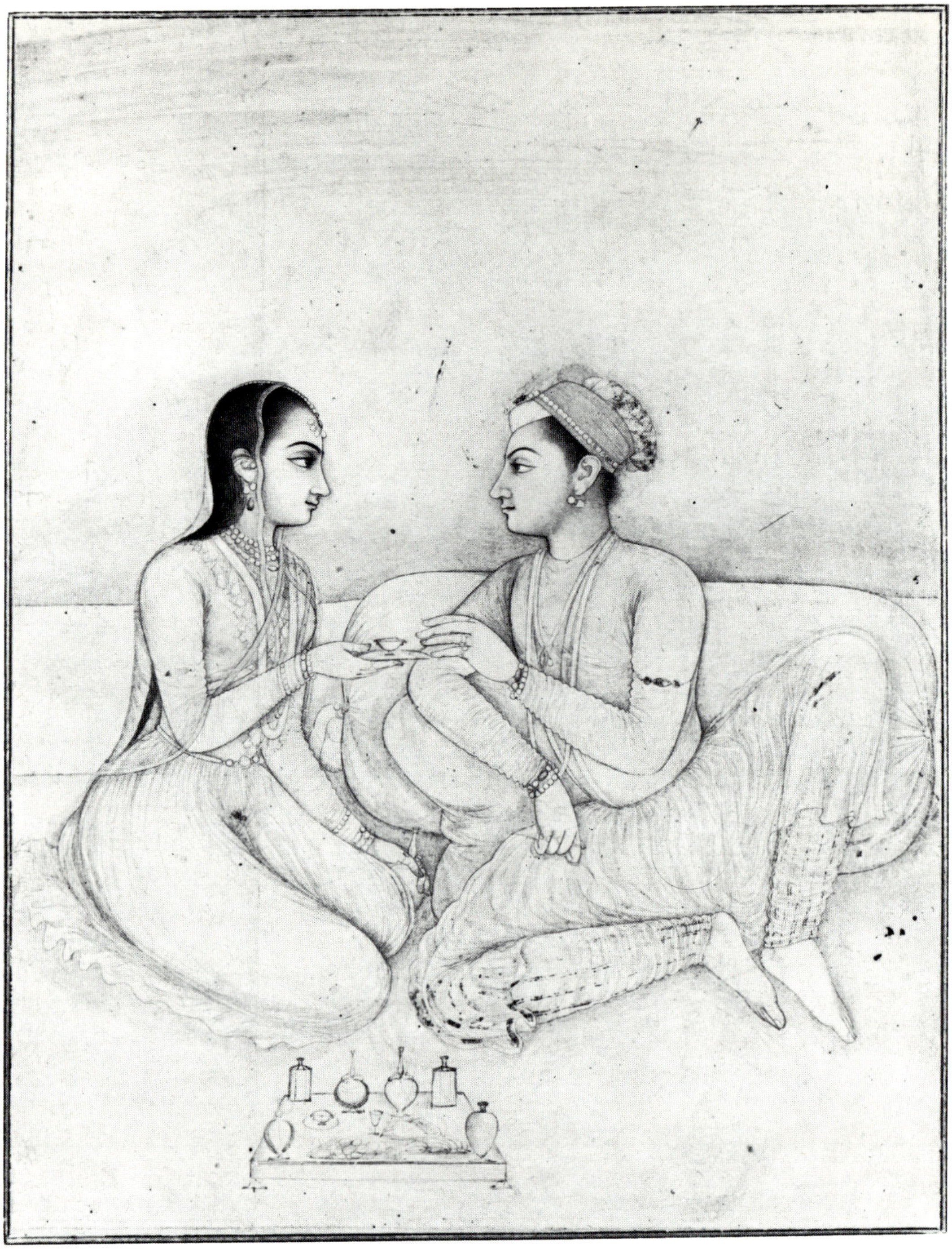

4 **A lady offers wine to her lover**
Mughal, *c* 1730
Drawing in brush and black ink, heightened with gold and touches of colour, on cream paper
Mounted on an album page with a calligraphy on the verso
243 × 186 mm; page 402 × 280 mm
Private collection

The double portrait of young lovers on a terrace, sharing a private moment, first appeared as a subject in Mughal art during the 1630s. Although paintings of this type might have had some matrimonial significance, this point is unclear. Whatever the pretext, the mood is often intensely romantic, and totally disarming, as it is here. TM

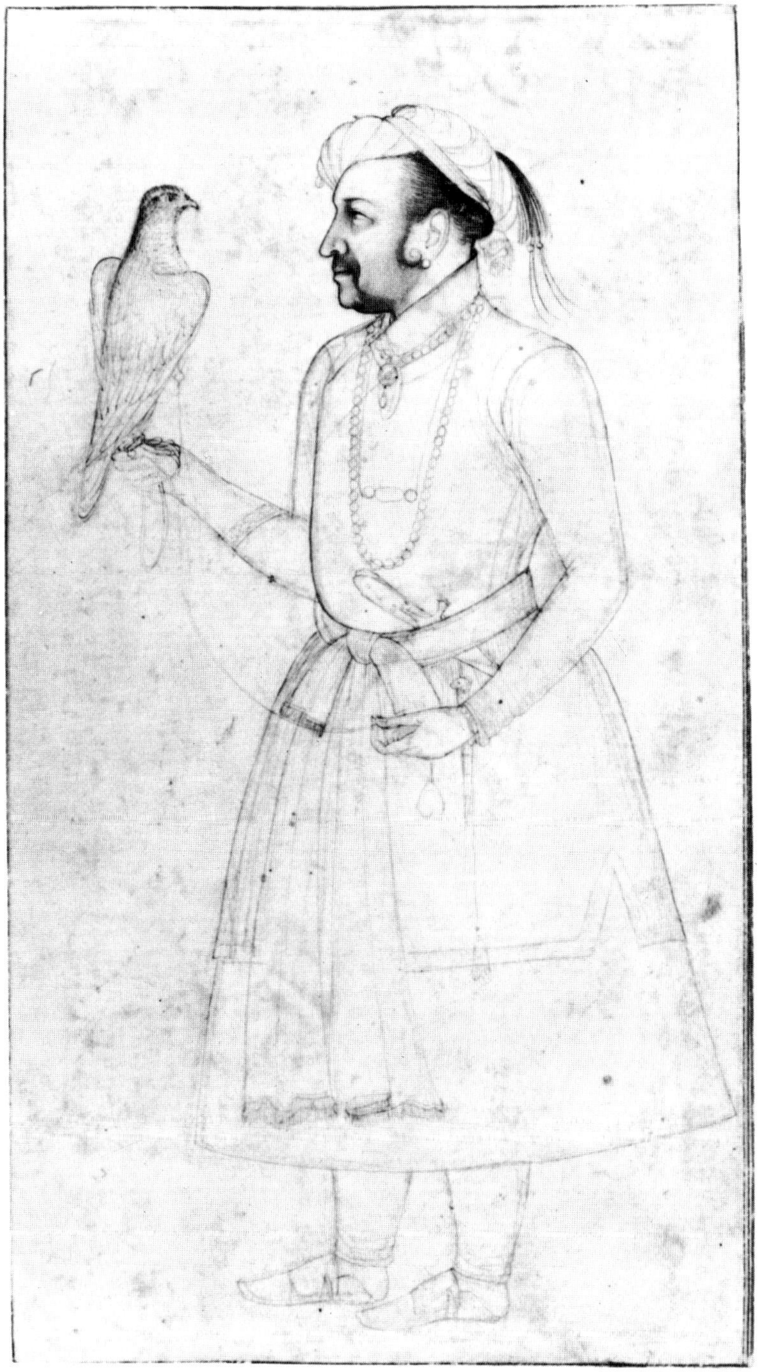

5 The Emperor Jahangir with a falcon

Attributed to Abu'l Hasan
Mughal, c 1620
Drawing in brush and black ink, heightened with touches of colour, on tan paper 180 × 98 mm
Literature: T. McInerney, 1982, no. 10
Private collection

Jahangir (r. 1605–27) was perhaps the greatest connoisseur of Indian painting; he was certainly one of the most discerning art collectors the world has seen. This portrait was drawn from life when the Emperor was about fifty-one. It was made by his favourite painter, Abu'l Hasan (fl. 1600–30), whom the art-loving monarch styled 'Nadir-al-Zaman', 'The Wonder of the Age'. Although Abu'l Hasan's full figure, profile representation is a standard convention, the obvious rapport between the artist and subject that is such a notable feature of this study is rarely attained in other imperial portraits of the same type. Indeed Jahangir is looking at the falcon, which is merely a symbol, or royal attribute, as if the bird actually meant something to him. TM

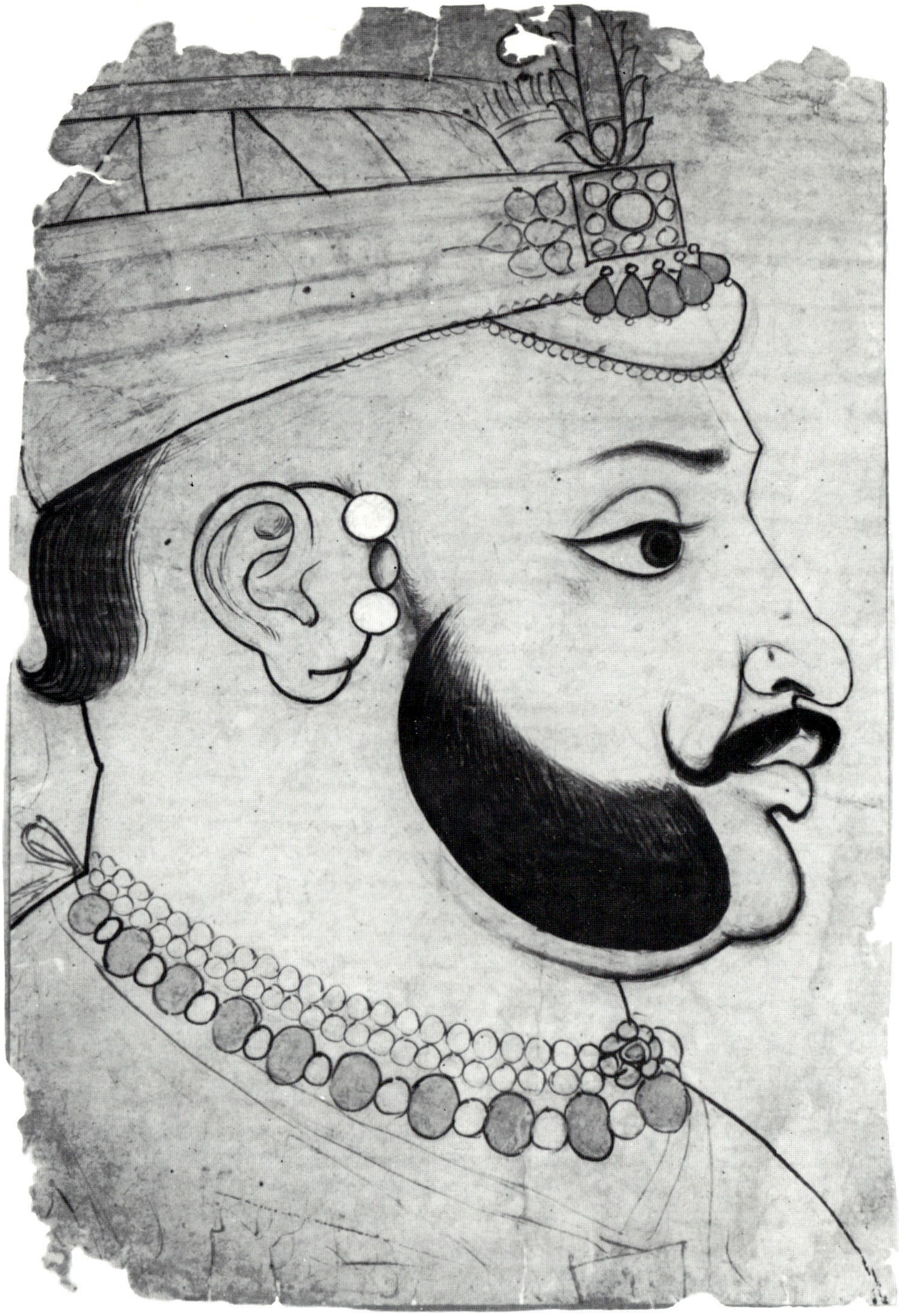

6 Ram Singh II of Kotah in profile

Rajasthan, Kotah School, *c* 1840
Drawing in brush and black ink, heightened with touches of white and colour, on brown paper 384 × 261 mm
Dr. Alvin Bellak

The size and scale of this drawing, as well as its technique, suggest that it was used as a cartoon, the finished design ready for transfer, for a wall painting. The thick, unwavering outlines, and the touches of colour on certain details, recall other Indian drawings that were certainly used in this way. Ram Singh II (r. 1828–66) was one of the most creative and engaging patrons of later Indian art. He wasn't much as a ruler, but he was quite intelligent and he liked to have fun. His wit and sly humour are certainly evident in this portrait. TM

7 Portrait of a Mughal Officer

Mughal, *c* 1660
Drawing in ink and brush, heightened with coloured washes
425 × 314 mm
Inscribed in Hindi: *Iltaphti Khan Amir Syah Jahani ('Iltaphti Khan, an officer of Shah Jahan')*
Literature: T. McInerney, 1982, no. 14
Private collection

This portrait drawn from life, has something of the patrician *sang-froid* which characterises the arts during Shah Jahan's reign, but its status is rather hard to determine. It has been described as a preparatory drawing for a miniature because of its scale, but this seems unlikely. HH

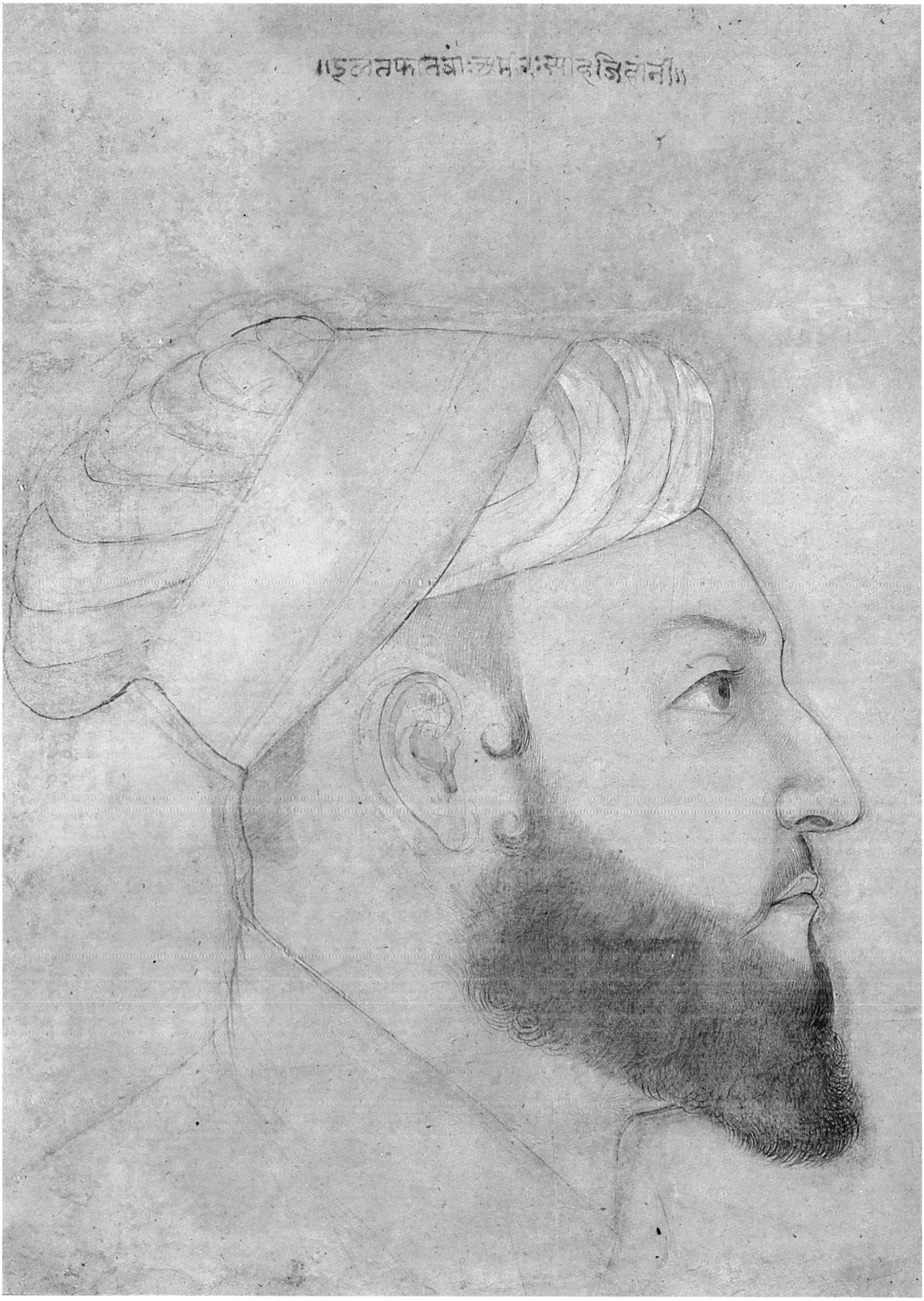

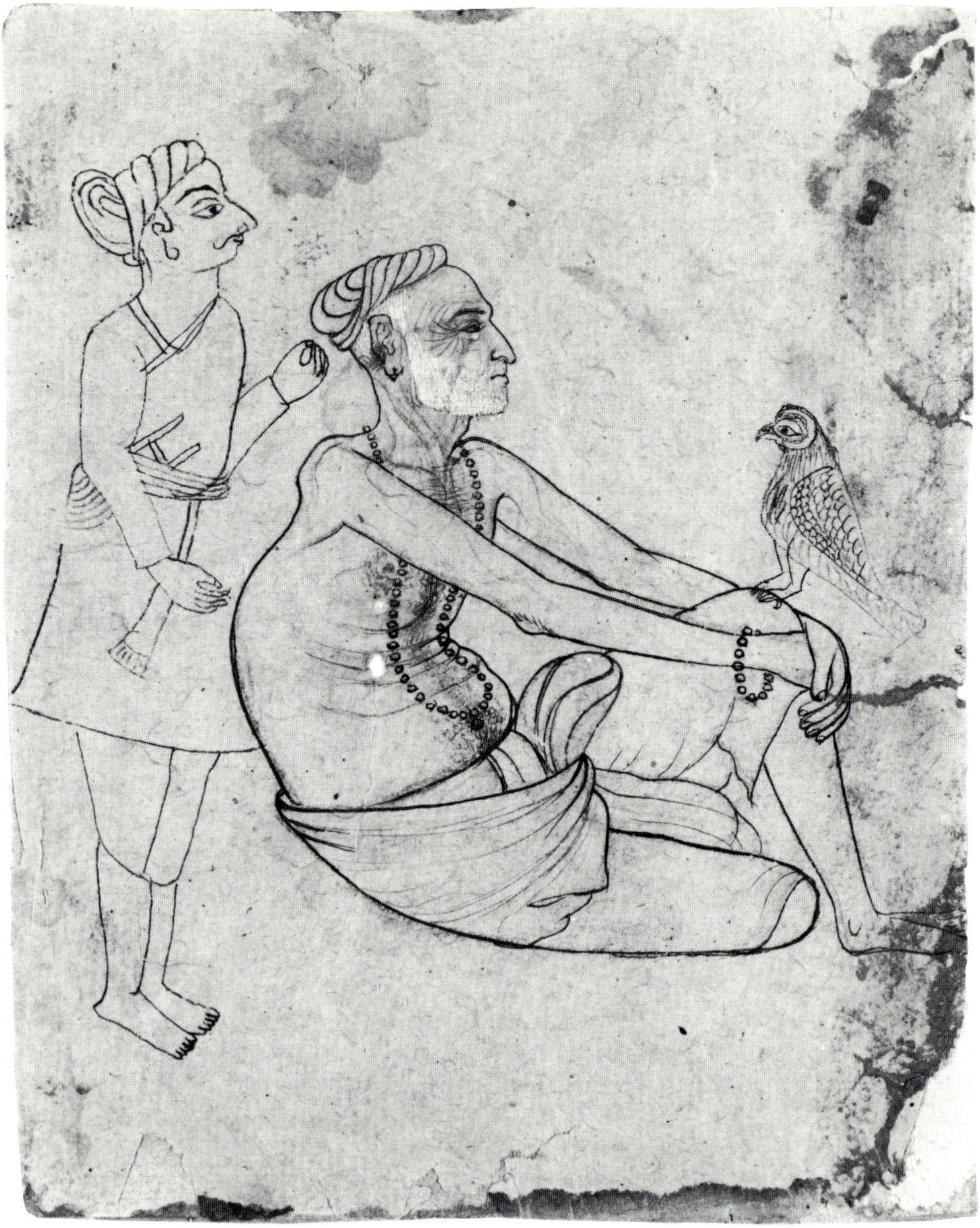

8 **Seated holy man**
Punjab Hills, *c* 1720
Brush drawing with white 224 × 180 mm
Private collection

This must be a study from direct observation, if not from life. The later additions from a childish hand – the figure on the left and the bird on the right – do not detract but rather by their clumsiness, accentuate the strength and sensitivity of the original drawing. HH

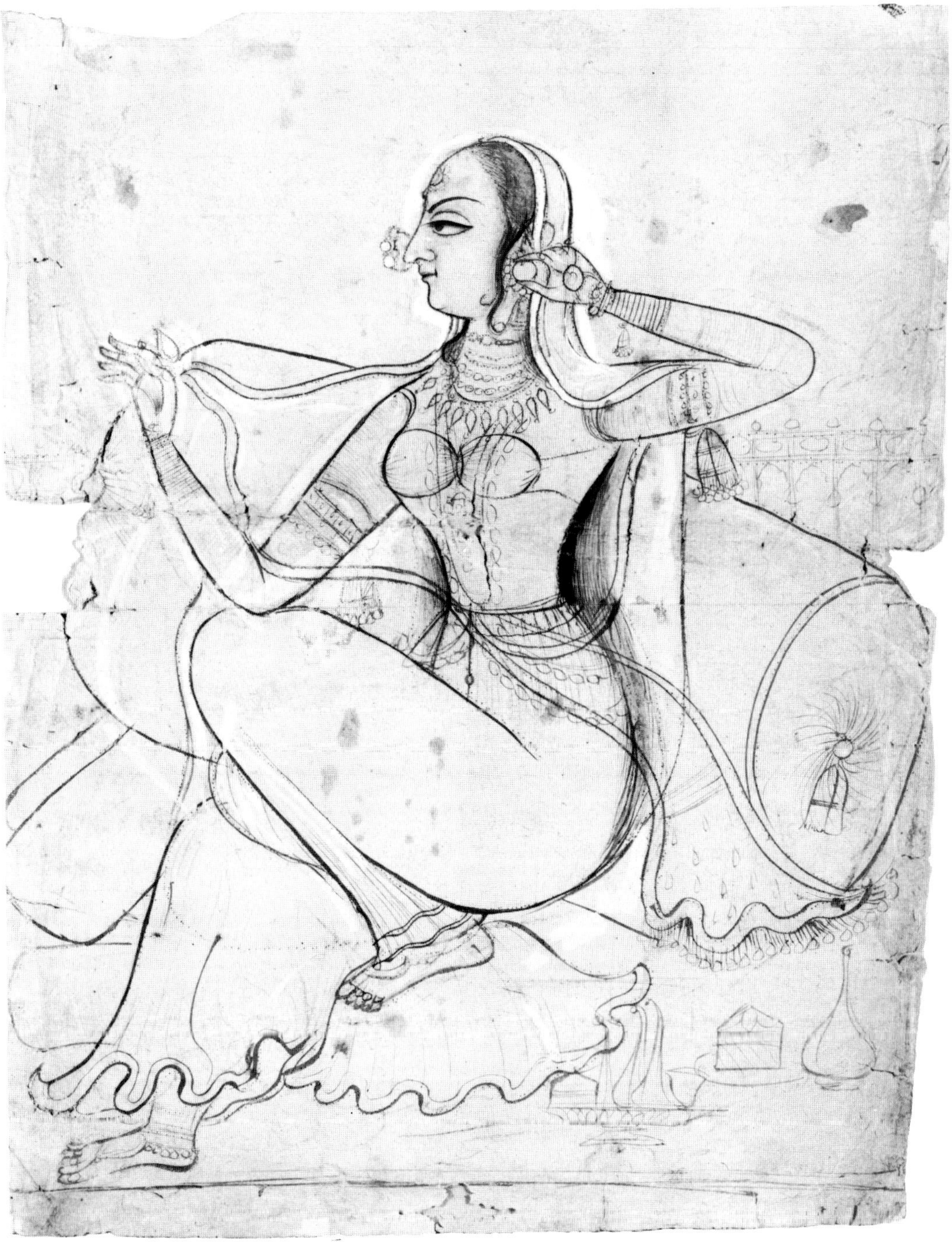

9 **A Courtesan**
Rajasthan, Jaipur, *c* 1780
Brush and black ink on paper 470 × 332 mm
Victoria & Albert Museum IS 315–1952, Gayer-Anderson Collection

A rather coarse drawing which doesn't depict anyone in particular it's more in the nature of a study for a pin-up. The ample, rather abstract curves anticipate the work of Jamini Roy, one of the founders of Modern Indian painting. HH

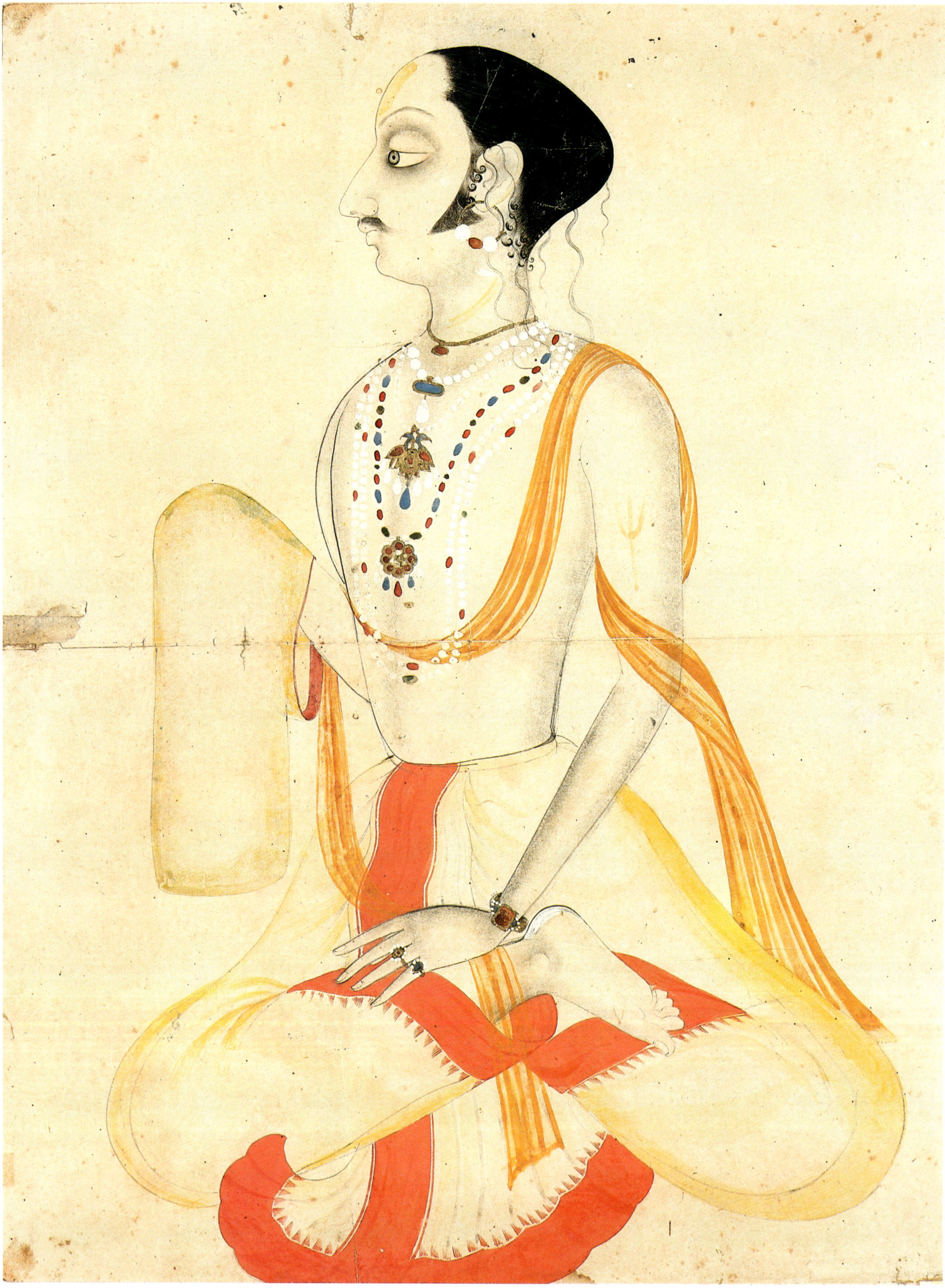

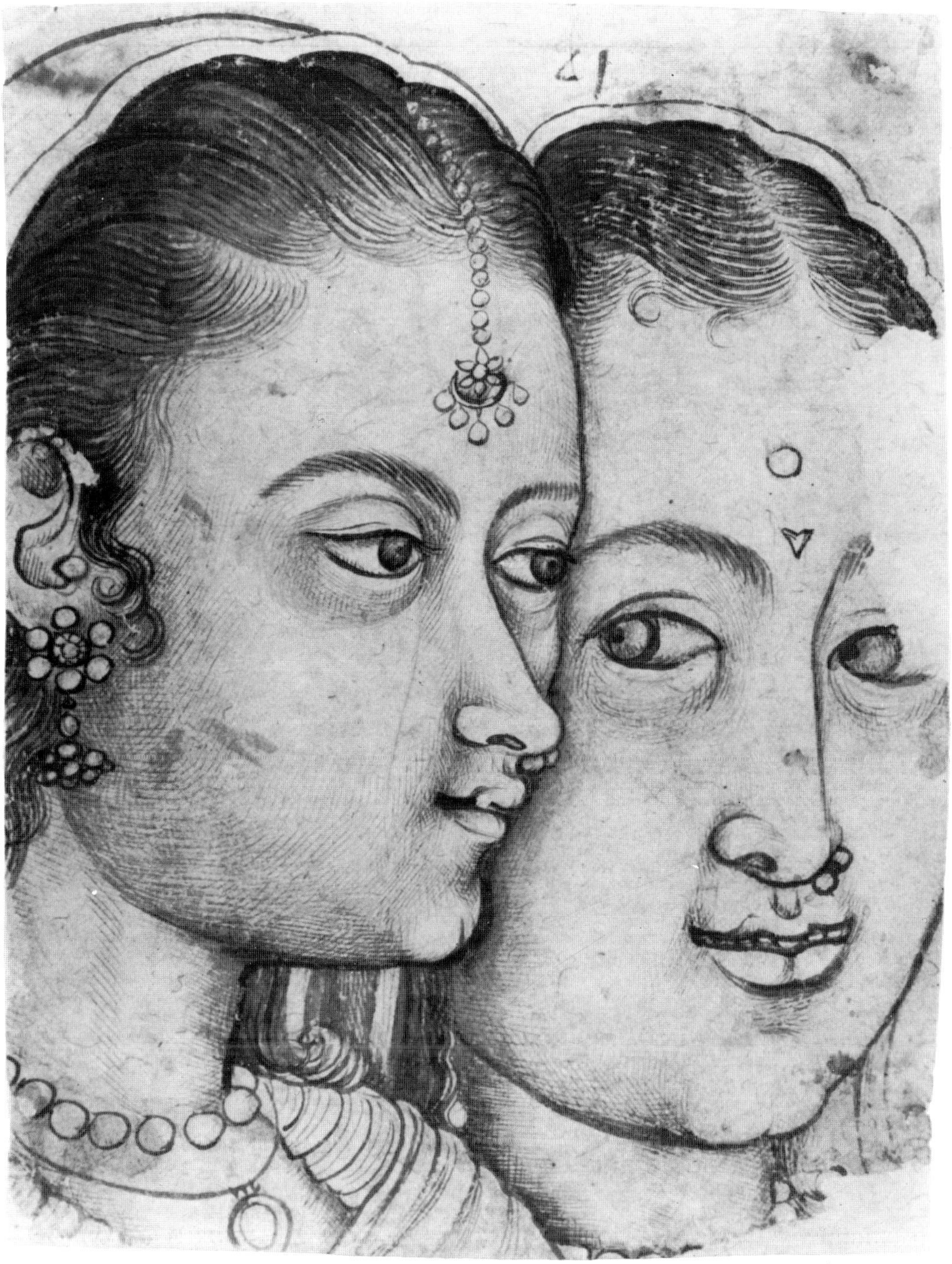

10 Rana Amar Singh II

Rajasthan, Mewar, *c* 1698
Black line with gold, colour and touches of white on paper
513 × 390 mm
Inscribed: *Maharaja Sri Raj Sri Amar Singhi doing japa at important worship*
Literature: S. C. Welch, 1976, no. 39
Private collection

This obviously idealised portrait which may at first glance look like a painting, is actually drawn with extraordinary finesse. For example, every hair in the moustache and on the head is separately delineated, and the colour plays a rather secondary rôle. HH

11 Two friends

Rajasthan, probably made at Jaipur, *c* 1775
Verso: the head of a girl in profile
Drawing in brush and black ink, heightened with touches of white, on brown paper (torn edges repaired) 197 × 145 mm (irregular)
Private collection

This drawing is neither a preliminary study, nor a finished work of art. It was probably made for the artist's own pleasure, to record a private moment, or to convey a particular feeling that he could not otherwise define. The mood is both tender and disturbing, as if the bond joining friend to friend involved pain as well as pleasure. TM

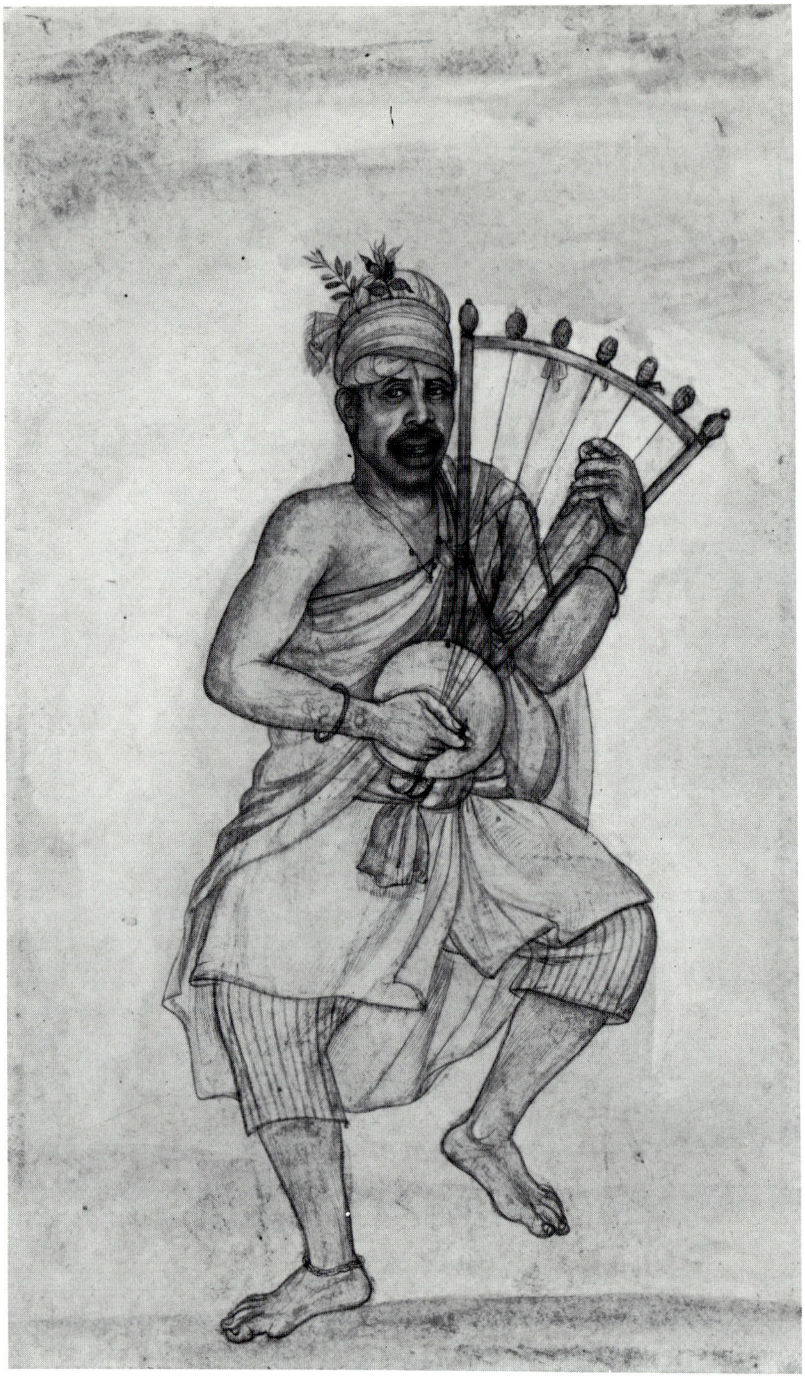

12 A Negro musician
Mughal, *c* 1650
Brush drawing 202 × 120 mm
Literature: A. Topsfield, 1980, no. 3
National Gallery of Victoria, Felton Bequest

This brilliant character study probably depicts an Abyssinian slave. We see him simultaneously singing, dancing and plucking his African lyre. The drawing has the immediacy of a photograph. HH

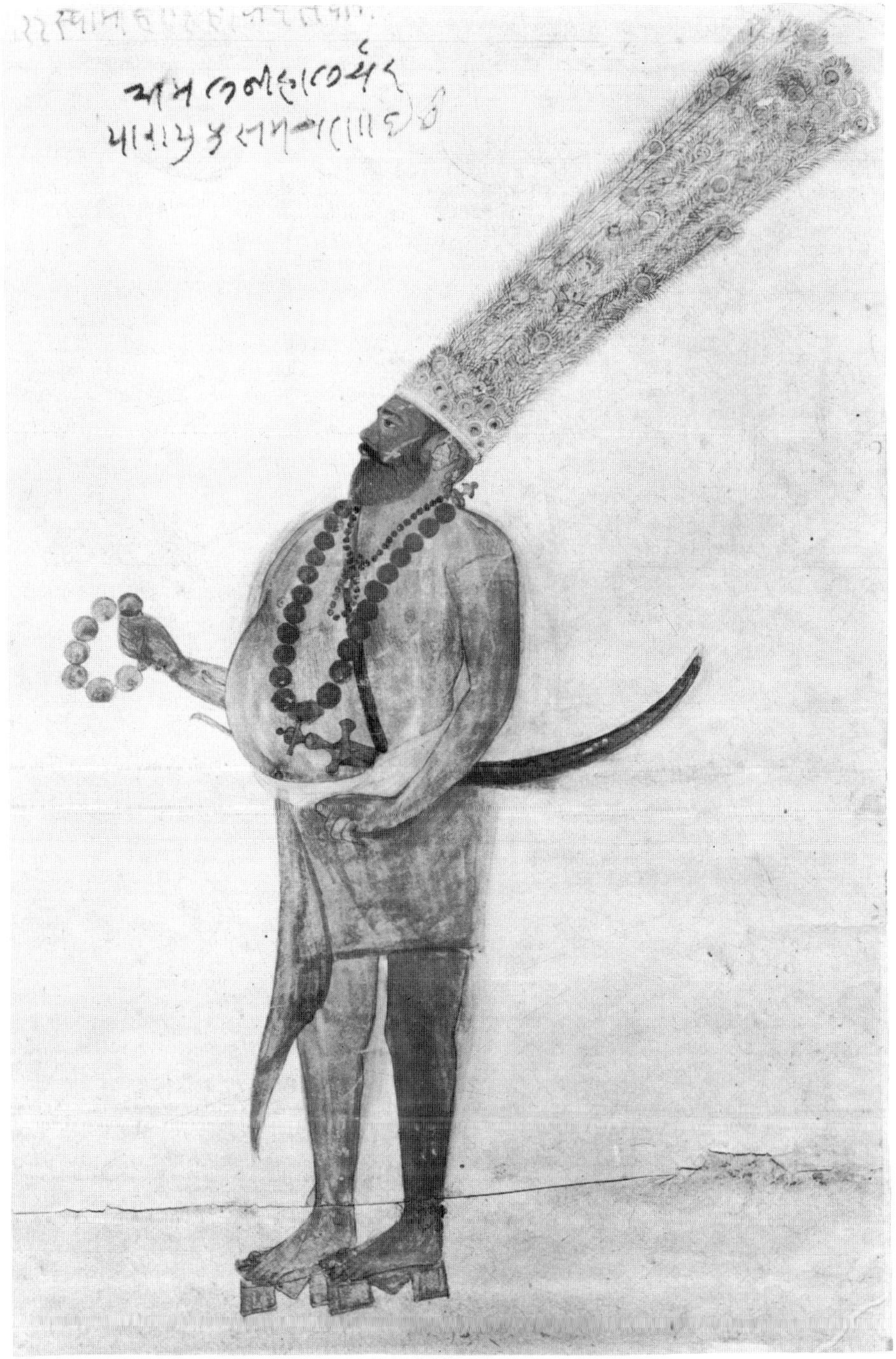

13 A Sadhu, or holy man, with a peacock crown
Nihal Chand
Rajasthan, Kishangarh School, *c* 1750
Drawing in brush and ink, heightened with colour and wax, on tan paper (torn and repaired) 258 × 174 mm
With a two line inscription in *nagari* characters, including an ascription to the artist
Dr. Alvin Bellak

Nihal Chand (fl. 1730–80) was the most famous painter of Kishangarh, a small yet important art centre in Rajasthan. He was renowned for his pictures of lovers dallying in vast landscapes, and for his original interpretations of the Krishna legends. Although his paintings are unquestionably visionary in intent, the present study suggests the degree of close observation that enriched and nourished his other more transcendental work, providing the naturalistic touchstone for his style. Nihal Chand was hardly an innocent, ignorant of the actual world: the note of wry humour found in this portrait is not only intentional, but apt. TM

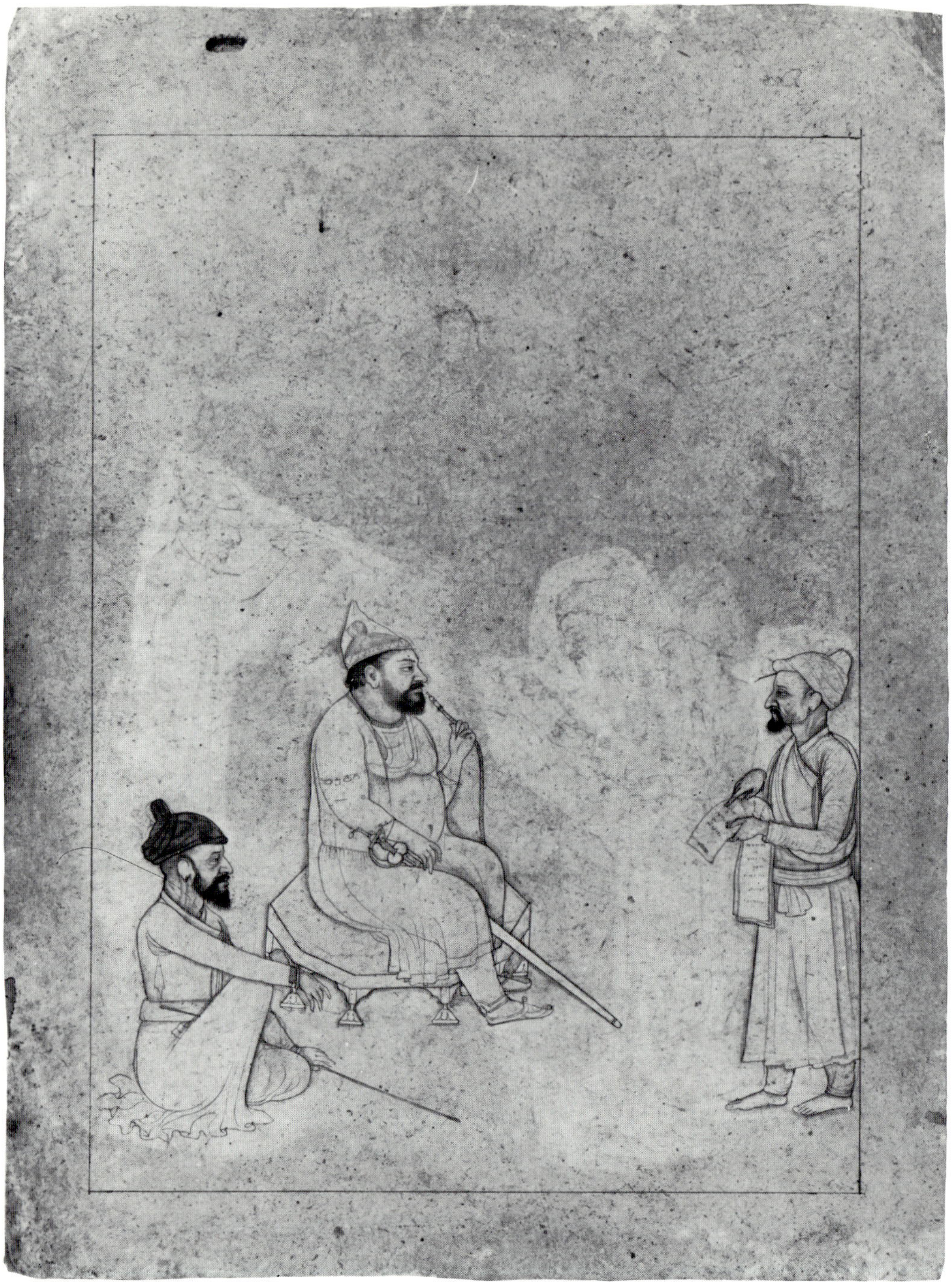

14 **Nobleman with attendants**

Punjab Hills, Guler, *c* 1750

Brush drawing on prepared ground 293 × 219 mm

Private collection

This profoundly sensitive drawing is a preparation for a painting. It shows particularly clearly how Indian artists corrected their work by overpainting in white. The ghostly outlines of other figures can still be seen in the background. HH

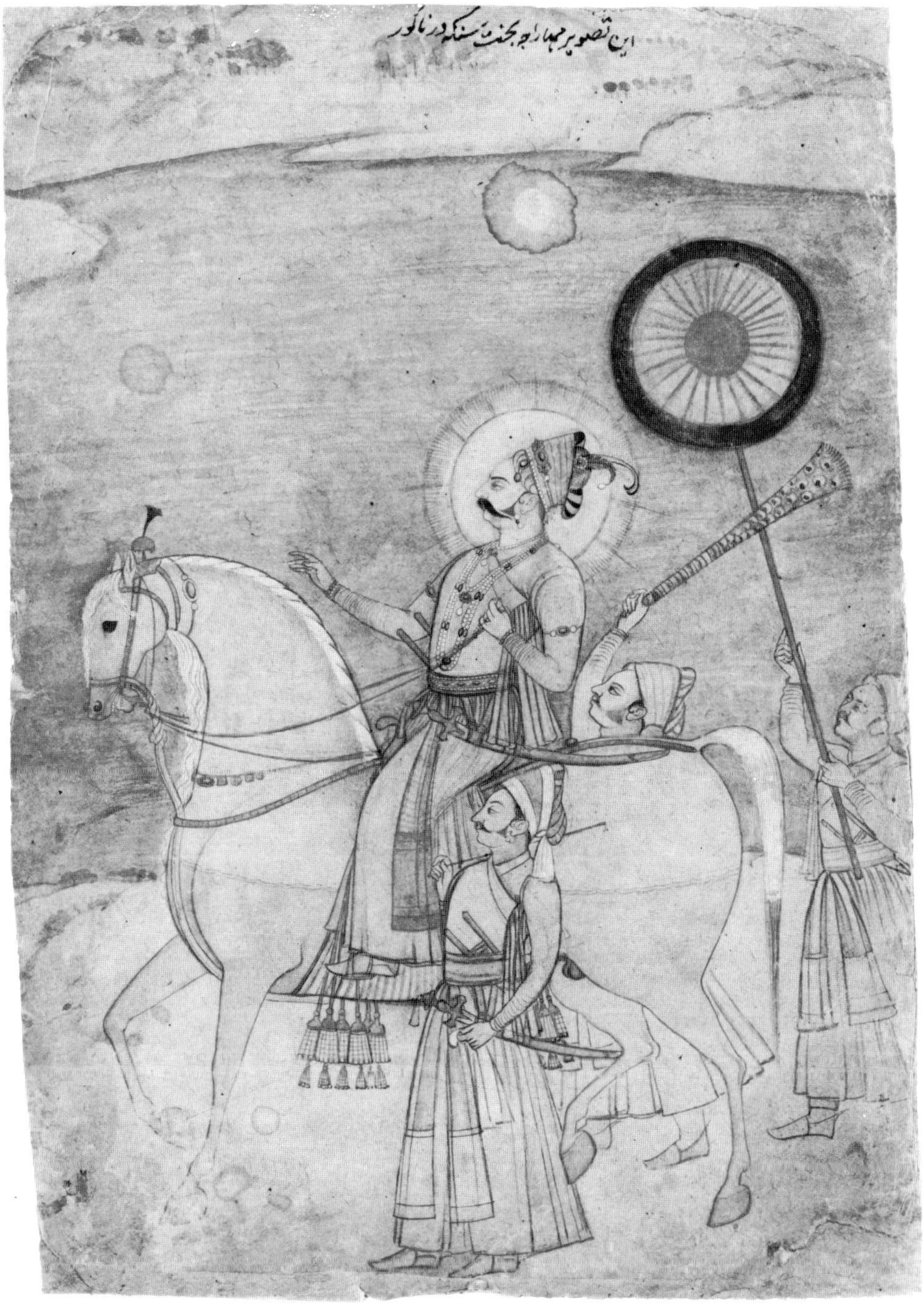

15 **Maharaja Bakht Singh of Jodhpur on horseback with attendants**

Rajasthan Bikaner, c 1751

Brush drawing, heightened with gold and colour, on paper

320 × 223 mm

Inscribed on recto and verso

Sven Gahlin

Inscribed, Maharaja Bakht Singh (1751–52) entering the city of Nagaur. Though the drawing was probably made at Bikaner, a second inscription, ascribing it to the seventeenth century Bikaner artist Ruknuddin, can probably be discounted, as he is unlikely to have continued working into the middle of the eighteenth century.

Though of unusually fine quality, this is an example of a stereotyped composition, of which painted versions exist in large numbers throughout Rajasthan. The source of this kind of equestrian portrait, which first appears in the seventeenth century, is probably European. HH

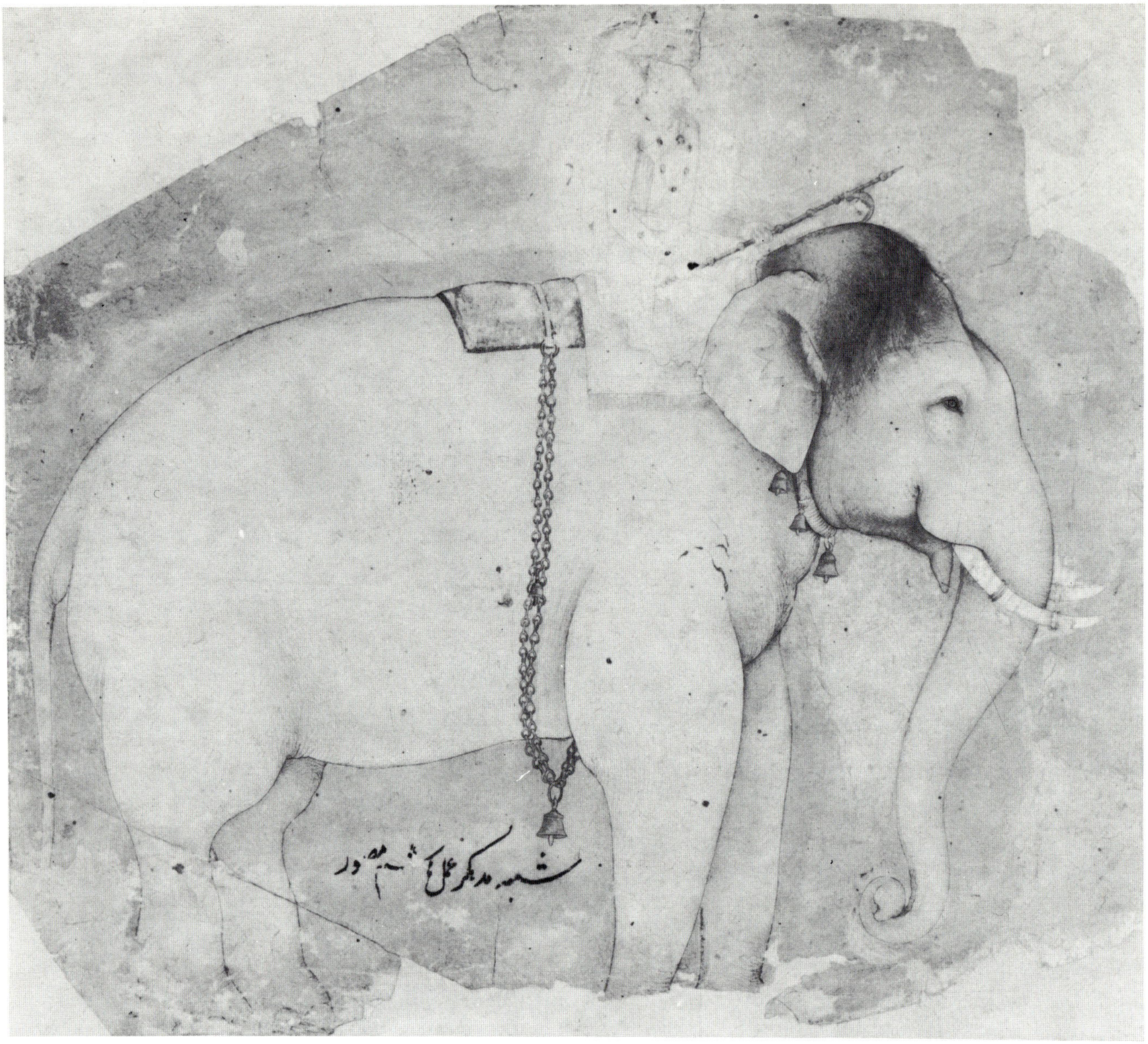

16 **Prince riding on an elephant**
Mughal *c* 1640
Line drawing enhanced with colour 209 × 235 mm
Inscribed: in the hand of Shah Jahan *by Hashim*
Fitzwilliam Museum, Cambridge

See note for no. 17.

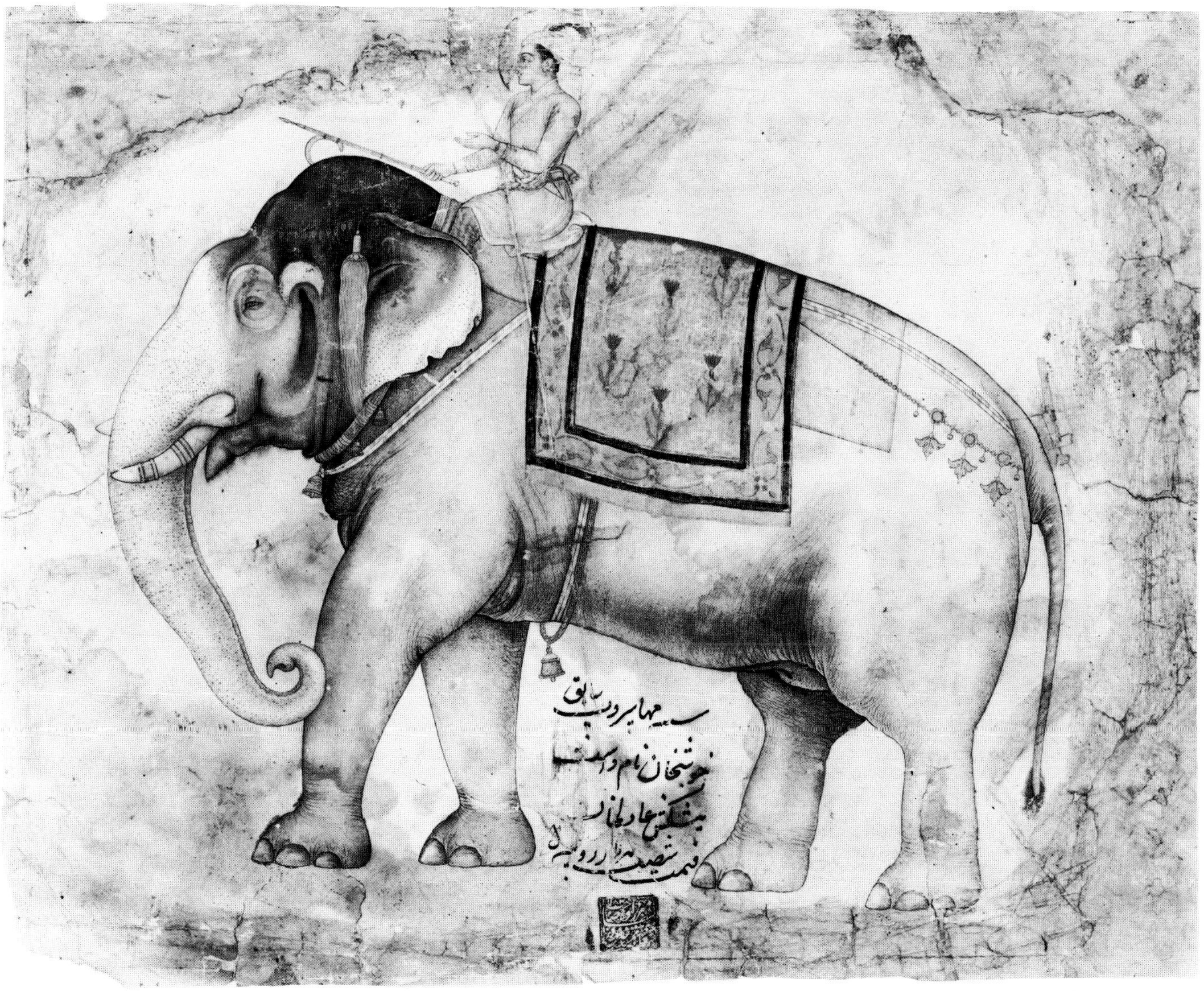

17 Portrait of the Imperial elephant Mahabir Deb

Mughal, school of Shah Jahan, *c* 1630

Brush drawing in ink, tinted with gold and watercolour on paper

325 × 405 mm

Inscribed by the Emperor Shah Jahan: '*Likeness of the Elephant, Mahabir Deb, previously named Khush Khan. Presented by Adil Shah. Value 300,000 rupees.*'

Literature: H. G. Rawlinson, 1947, pl. XI; Philip Rawson, 1972, pp. 136–137

Victoria & Albert Museum IM 23–1928, given by R. S. Green-Shields, 1928

Elephants had a unique position at the Mughal Court. They were loved, admired, doted on; and given as the grandest of presents. They were symbols of beauty and might. Not surprisingly, this drawing and no. 16, both portraits from the Imperial Collection, are the work of great artists, though precise attributions are as yet uncertain. IIII

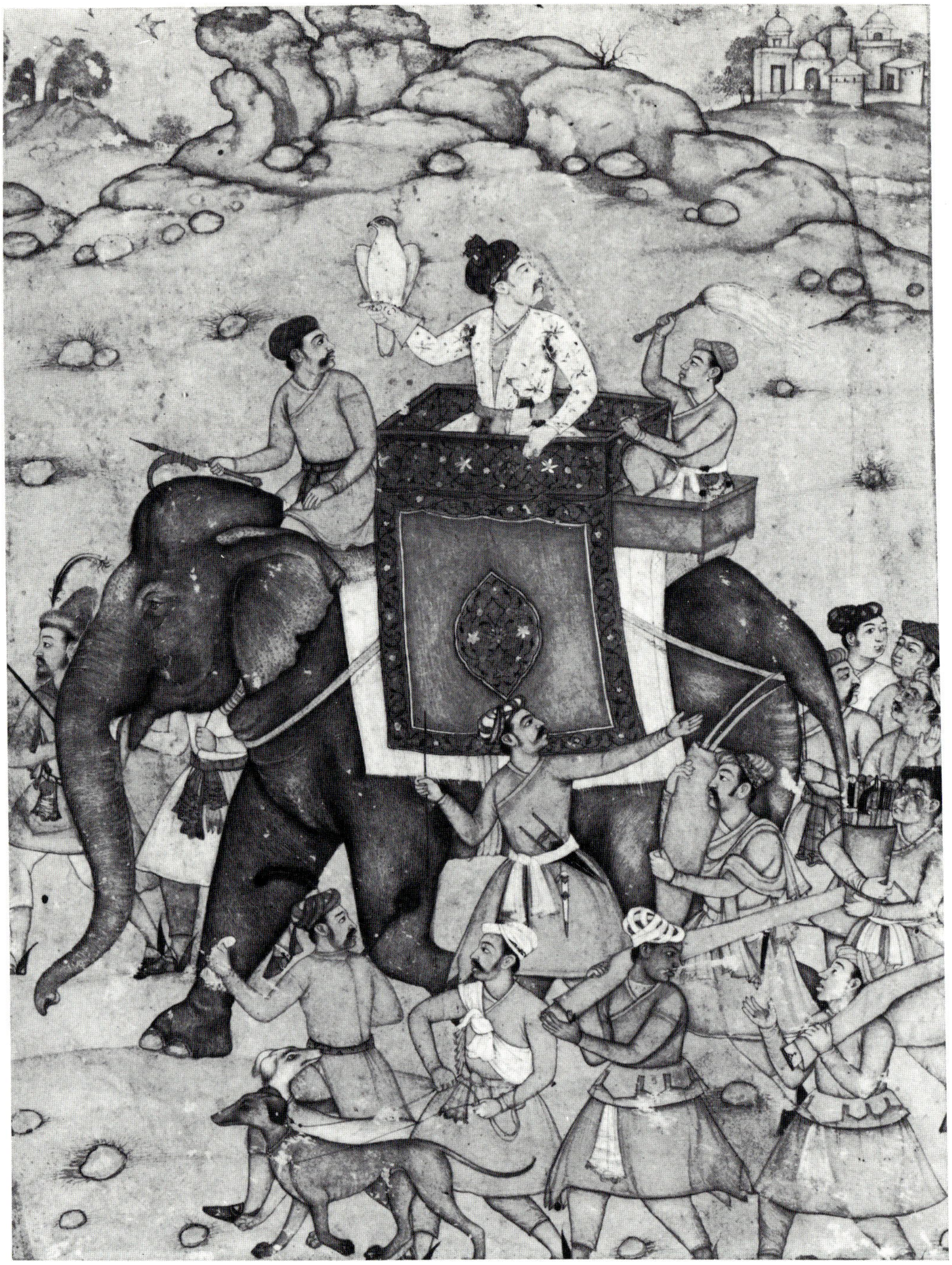

18 The Emperor Akbar the Great (1556–1605) hunting from a howdah borne on the back of an elephant

Mughal, Delhi school, early seventeenth century
Brush drawing, watercolour and gold on paper 175 × 135 mm; page 395 × 292 mm
Victoria & Albert Museum IM 249–1921

This drawing is technically interesting as it comes close to being a painting, or rather, the equivalent of a European watercolour. It is related in style to certain pages of the Chester Beatty *Akbar Nama* *c* 1605 and in particular to the work of the artist Sur Das, to whom it has been attributed by Robert Skelton, though it lacks energy compared to the better works of the period. HH

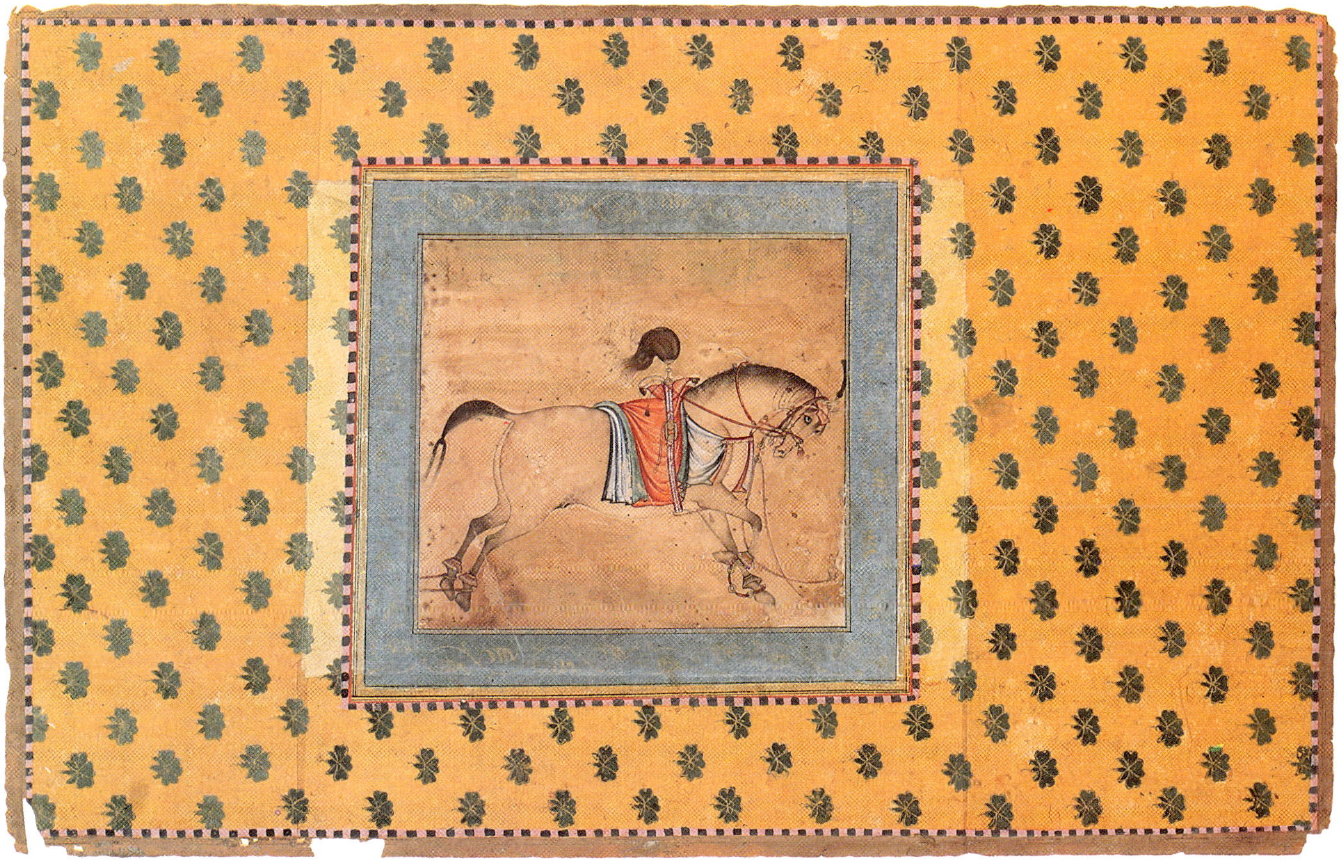

19 **A tethered horse**
Mughal, *c* 1650
Brush drawing, heightened with colour, on paper 100 × 112 mm
Sven Gahlin

Presumably a portrait of a royal favourite, in this case a horse. Though filled with life in every detail, note particularly the splendid black plume, it is most unlikely to have been drawn from nature, and the painted saddle cloth is simply conventional drapery. HH

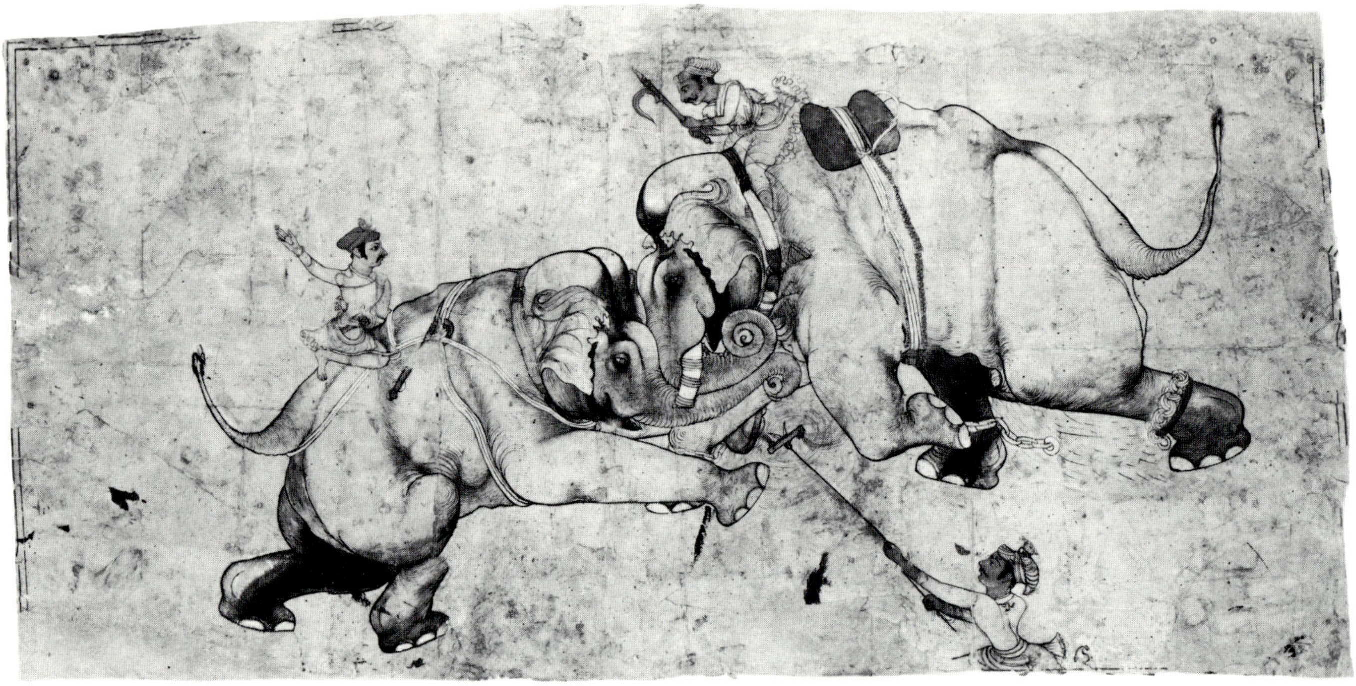

20 An elephant combat

Rajasthan, Kotah School, late seventeenth century
Brush and black ink, heightened with colours and touches of white, on paper 343 × 674 mm
Literature: L. Ashton, 1949, no. 484; M. C. Beach, 1974, pl. LXXI, fig. 75; S. C. Welch, 1976, no. 44
Private collection

This drawing is one of the finest of its kind to survive. The design of the two conjoined heads and trunks is an extraordinary invention which speaks for itself. It is worth noting that though the sheet is damaged (fragments of the border exist on all four sides) the dramatic composition, with the cut off figure in the foreground, follows the original intentions of the artist and is not the result of cutting. HH

21 Prince Khurram embracing his father, Jahangir

Mughal, *c* 1630
Drawing with gouache and gold in places; 296 × 208 mm; page 411 × 266 mm
Literature: A. K. Coomaraswamy, 1910, pl. II; P. Brown, 1924, pl. LVIII; A. K. Coomaraswamy, 1927, 292–93; J. S. Wilkinson, 1948, pl. 7; S. C. Welch, 1976, no. 18
British Library, India Office Library and Records

The Emperor Jahangir and Prince Khurram (later Shah Jahan) embrace before gathered courtiers. The Emperor has left his position in the centre of the balcony to meet Prince Khurram, and a single courtier stands in the equivalent position on the right of the throne. Jahangir's courtiers are gathered in two crowds in the courtyard beneath, and an elephant is in the right foreground with the rider saluting.

Apparently this is a preparatory drawing for the illustration of Prince Khurram's return to Ajmer in 1614, which is on folio 42 of the manuscript of the Shah Jahan Nama (Annals of Shah Jahan) in the collection of Her Majesty the Queen at Windsor Castle.

The inscription in part reads: *portraits of the Emperor Jahangir and Shah Jahan at the time of their departure for Balkh.* Though presumably not by the artist Manohar, to whom it is attributed in an early inscription, this drawing must be by one of the greatest Mughal painters of the period. HH

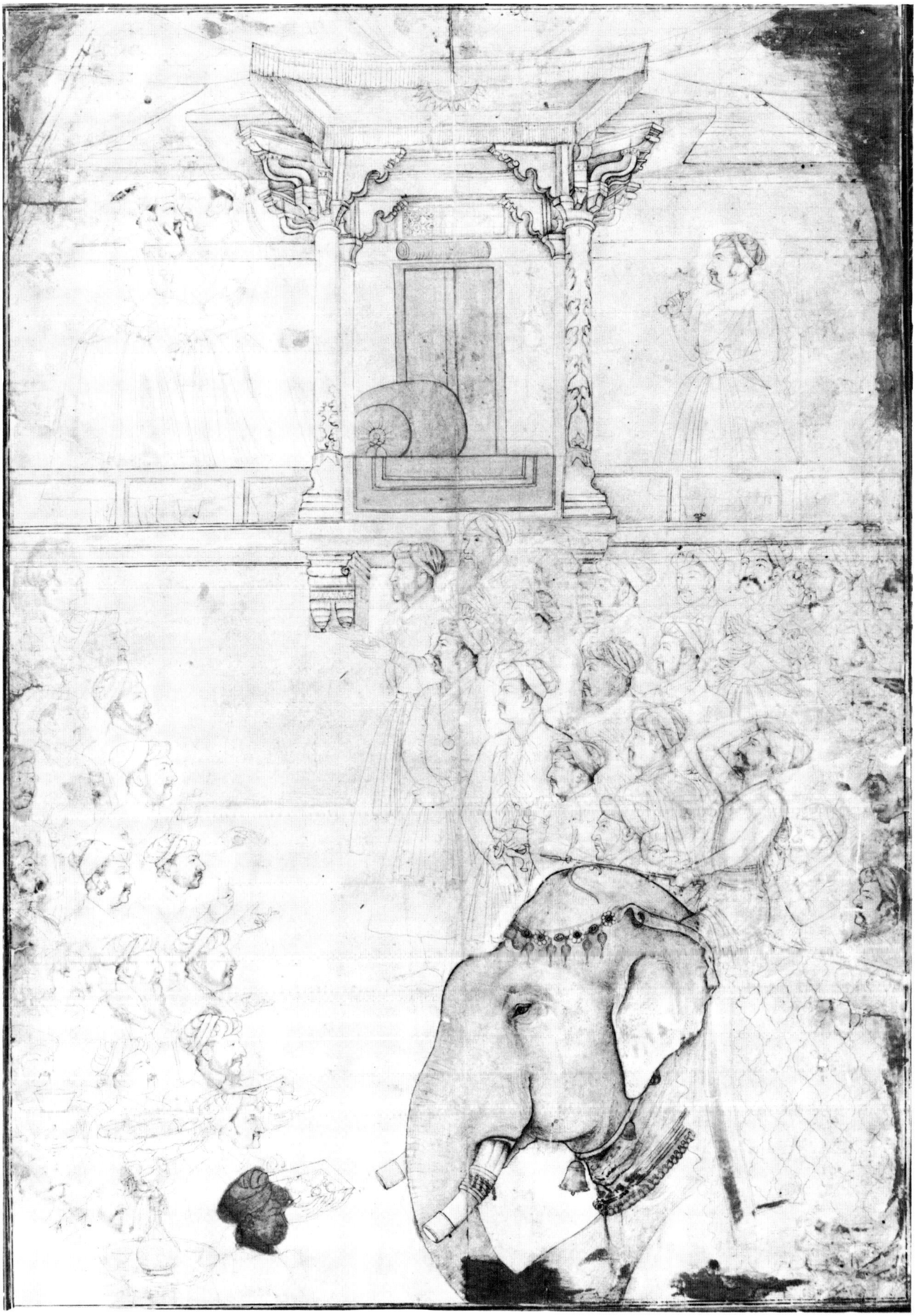

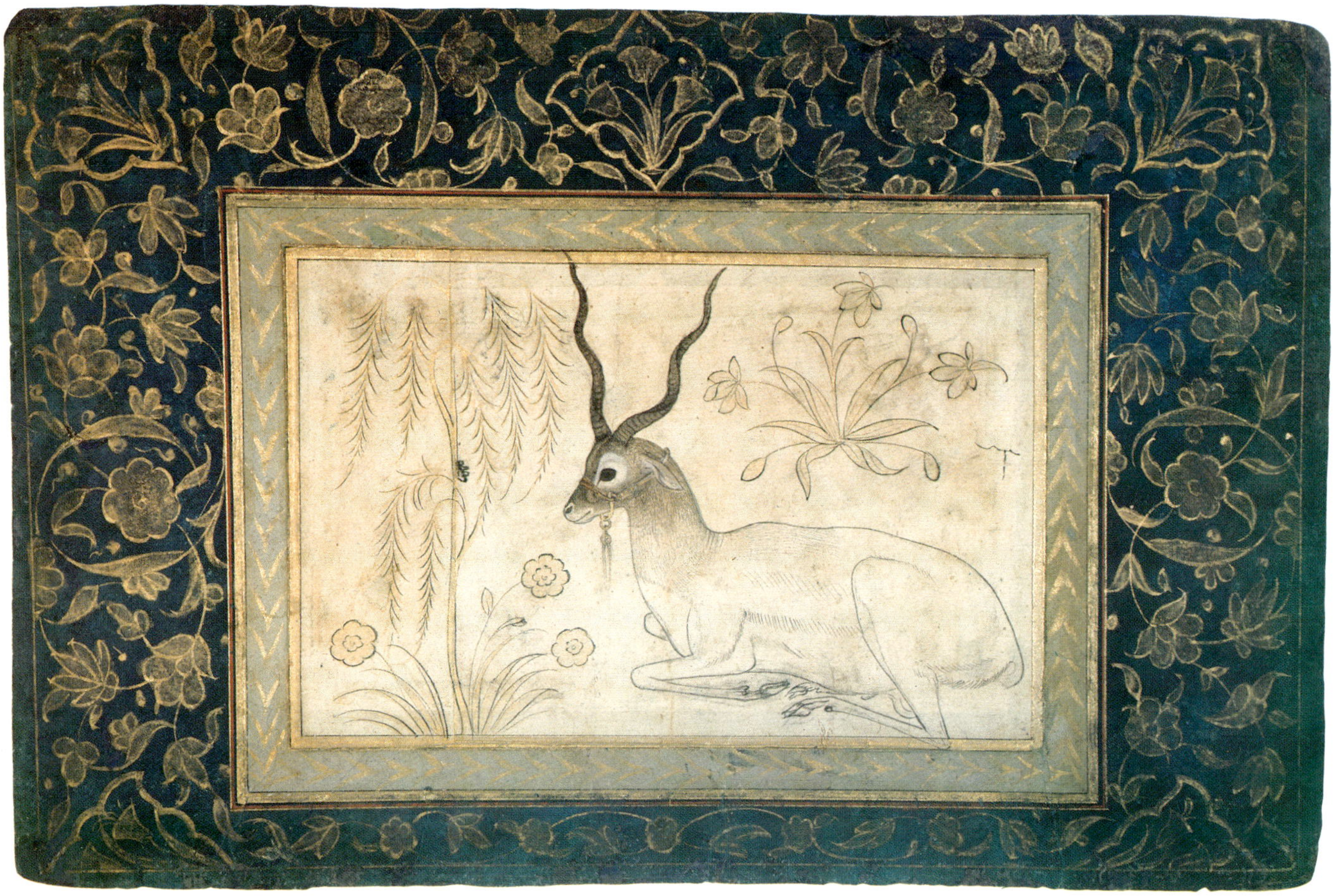

22 A seated antelope
Attributed to Mansur
Mughal, *c* 1630
Brush drawing in black ink and gold, heightened with touches of white and colour, on cream paper
Dark blue margins decorated with floral arabesques in gold (corner repaired) 120 × 191 mm; page 223 × 342 mm
Private collection

This work relates to a particularly distinctive type of Mughal court drawing: the marginal illuminations in gold and silver, those refined studies of flora and fauna, that decorate the borders of imperial albums and other deluxe manuscripts of various types. This connection is established by the cursive underdrawing in gold that one can easily discern beneath the flowers and tree. These were probably added once the antelope had been finished. This remarkably sensitive animal was undoubtedly drawn by Mansur (fl. 1590–1640), who was the greatest of Mughal animal painters, as well as a famous illuminator in gold. Many Indian animal studies of a certain quality are attributed to Mansur as a matter of course; but this one seems right. He probably began this sketch from life (note the pentimenti beneath the legs), and revised it later as a finished, autonomous work. He would have added the flowers and tree at this stage. They heighten the tone of limpid spirituality, and imbue the antelope with the painterly equivalent of physical breath.

Prof. S. C. Welch first suggested the attribution to Mansur. For other animal studies by the same artist, see M. C. Beach, 1978, pp. 137–143.

TM

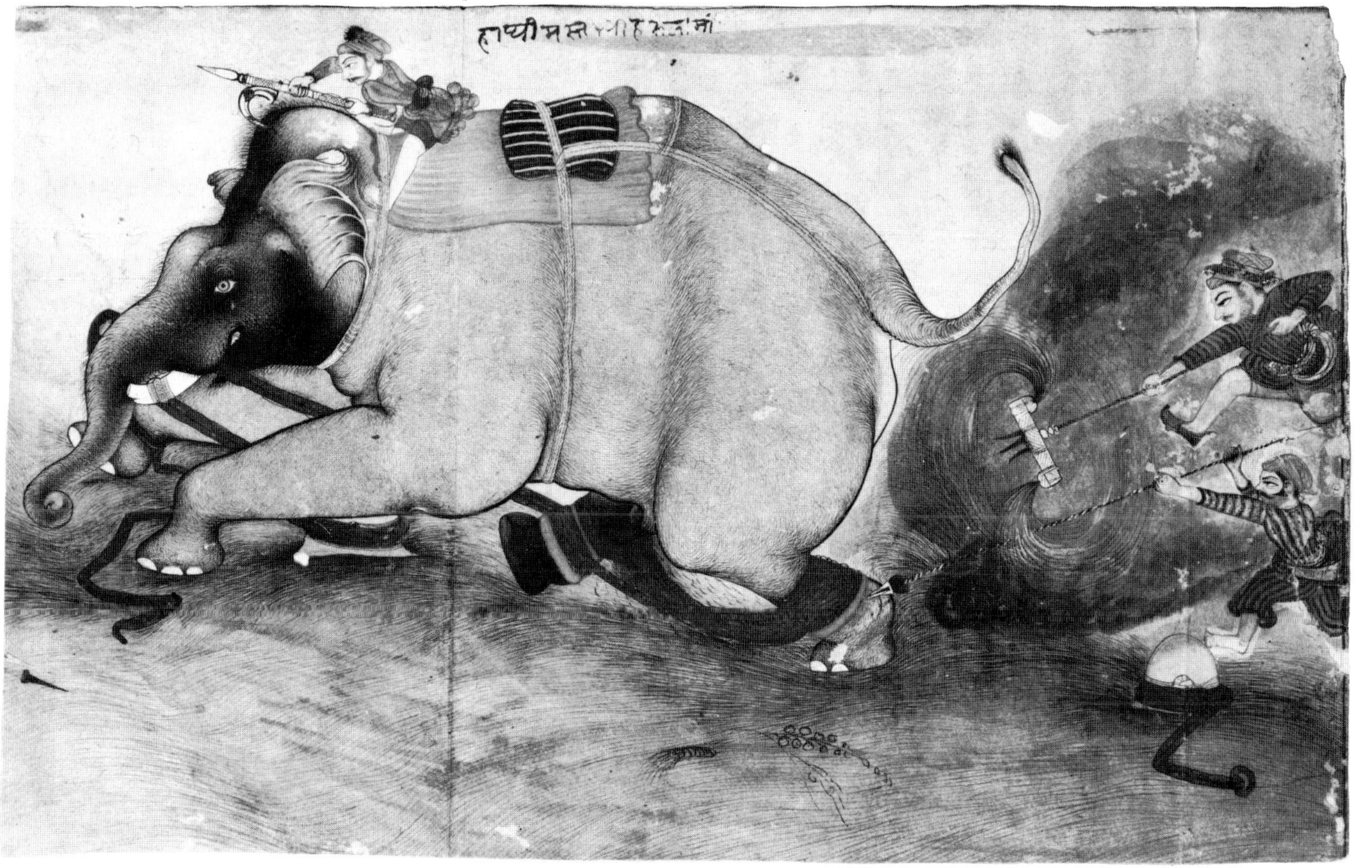

23 Elephant being excited by fireworks
Rajasthan, Kotah, late seventeenth century
Brush drawing with colour and silver 235 × 381 mm
Private collection

This elaborately finished drawing was finally tinted with transparent colour. The leg-bindings of the elephant were once silver which has now oxidized to black.

HH

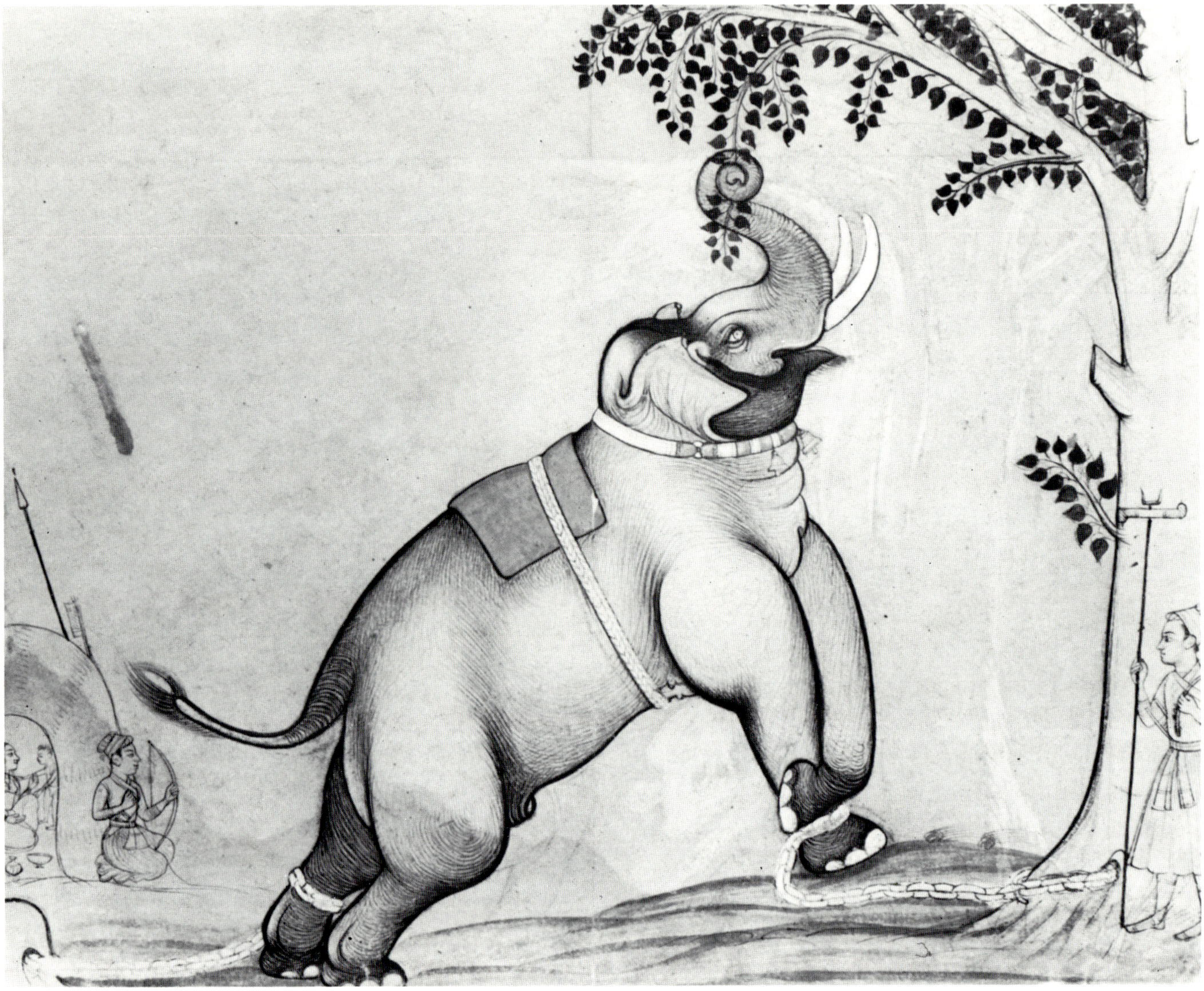

24 An elephant tied to a pipal tree

Rajasthan, Ajmer School, *c* 1725

Brush drawing in orange and black ink, heightened with broad areas of colour, on tan paper 340 × 426 mm

Private collection

The elephant is tied to a pipal tree, the leaves of which are extremely bitter. This vigorous, coloured drawing probably illustrates a moralising tale derived from folklore. TM

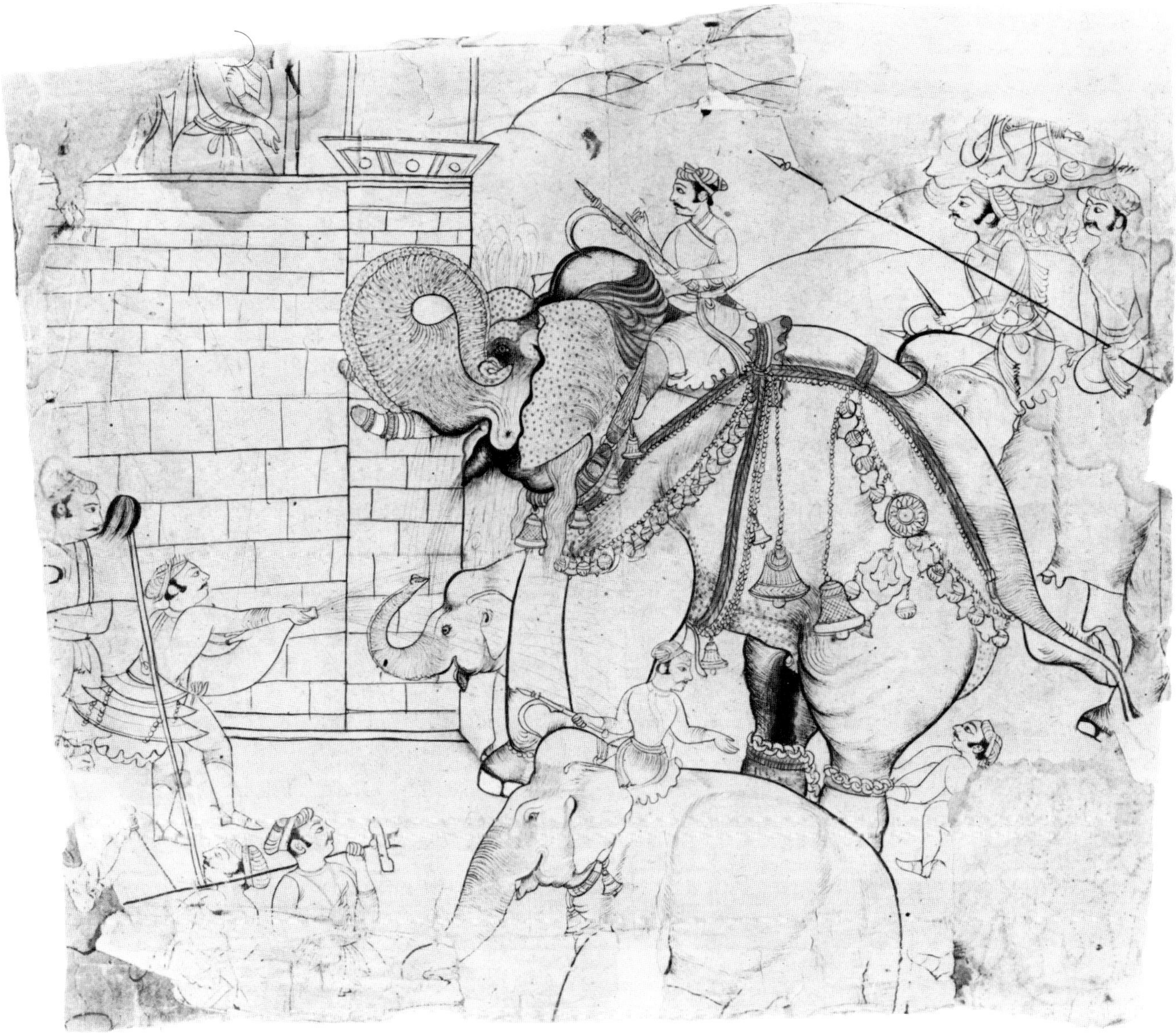

25 **Elephant outside a citadel**
Rajasthan, Kotah, mid seventeenth century
Brush drawing 241 × 280 mm
Literature: M. C. Beach, 1974, fig. 81, pl. 76
Private collection

This drawing is unique and although presumably made at Kotah, no exact parallels have been found. The central elephant is a magnificent warlike image, but the drawing does contain variations in style, which make precise dating and attribution difficult. HH

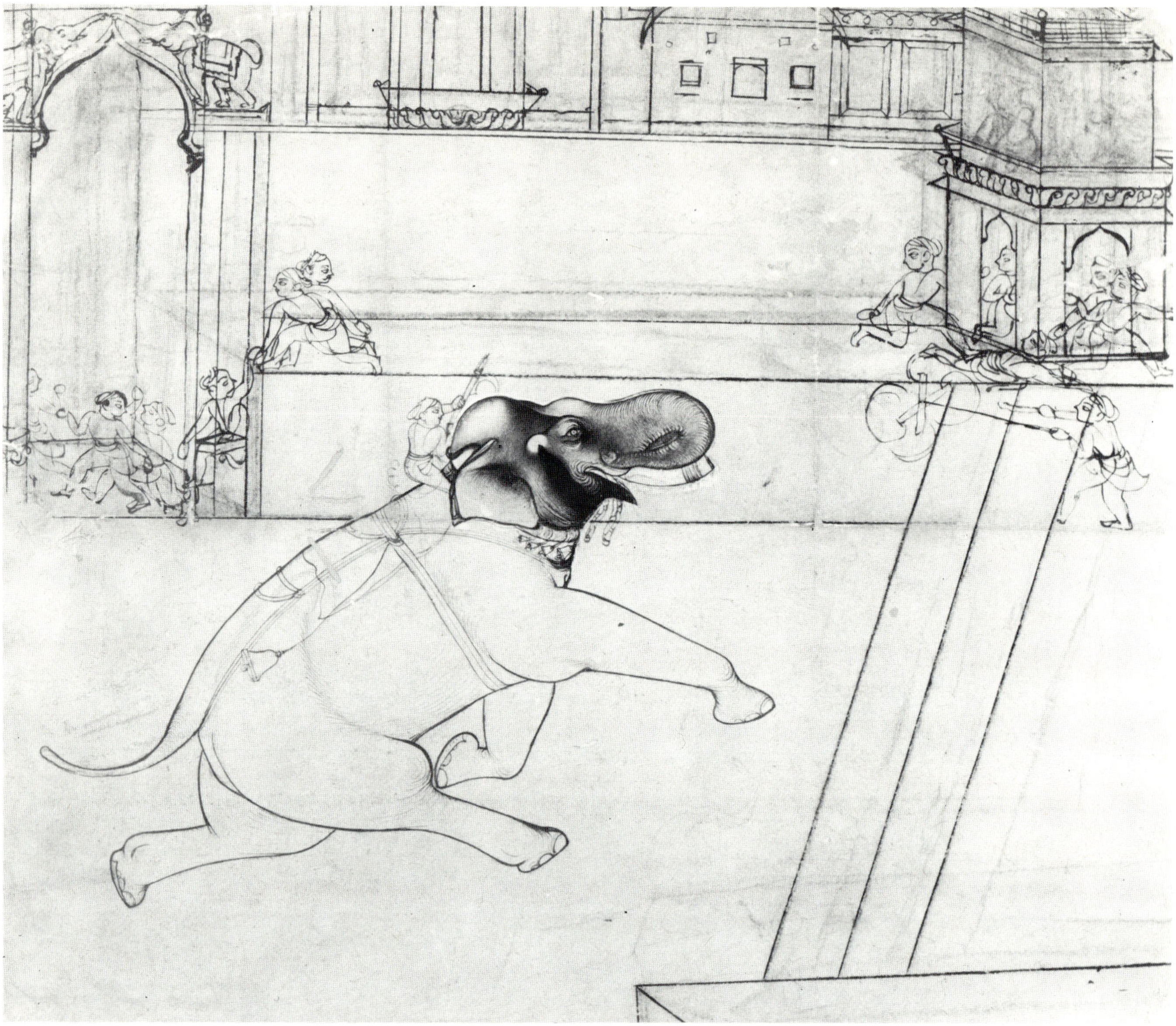

26 **A charging elephant**
Rajasthan, Kotah school, early eighteenth century
Brush drawing, black, brown inks, heightened with white, underdrawing in black chalk 483 × 559 mm
Robert and Lisa Sainsbury Collection, University of East Anglia

Probably made in preparation for a painting and in that sense perhaps a finished work, as the detailed study of the head would set the style for the rest of the picture. HH

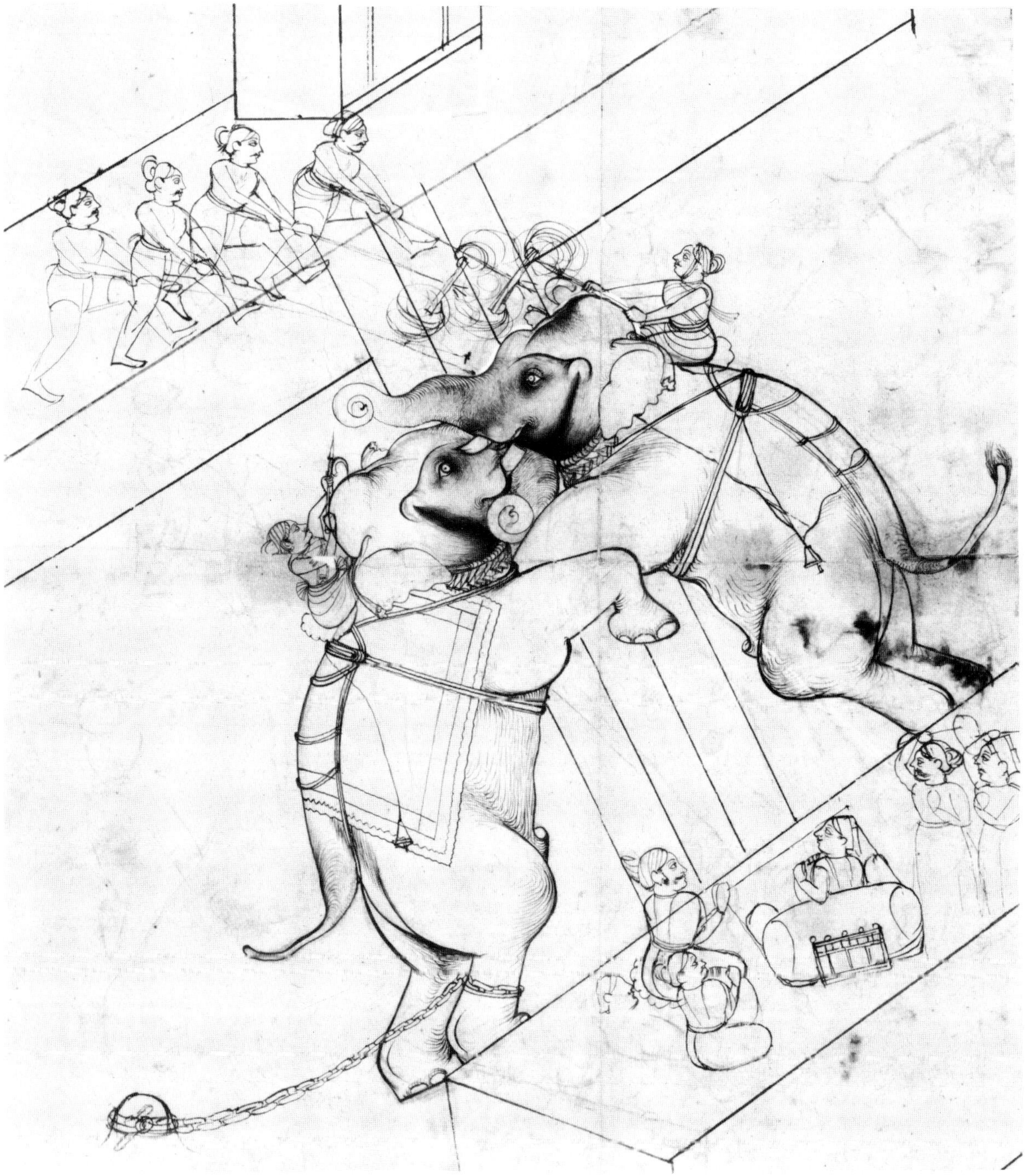

27 Elephants fighting
Rajasthan, Kotah, *c* 1750
Brush drawing 437 × 406 mm
Lisbet Holmes

This is another preparatory study for a painting. The deformations of the elephant's trunks are reminiscent of a more finished drawing (See no. 23), though not necessarily by the same hand. HH

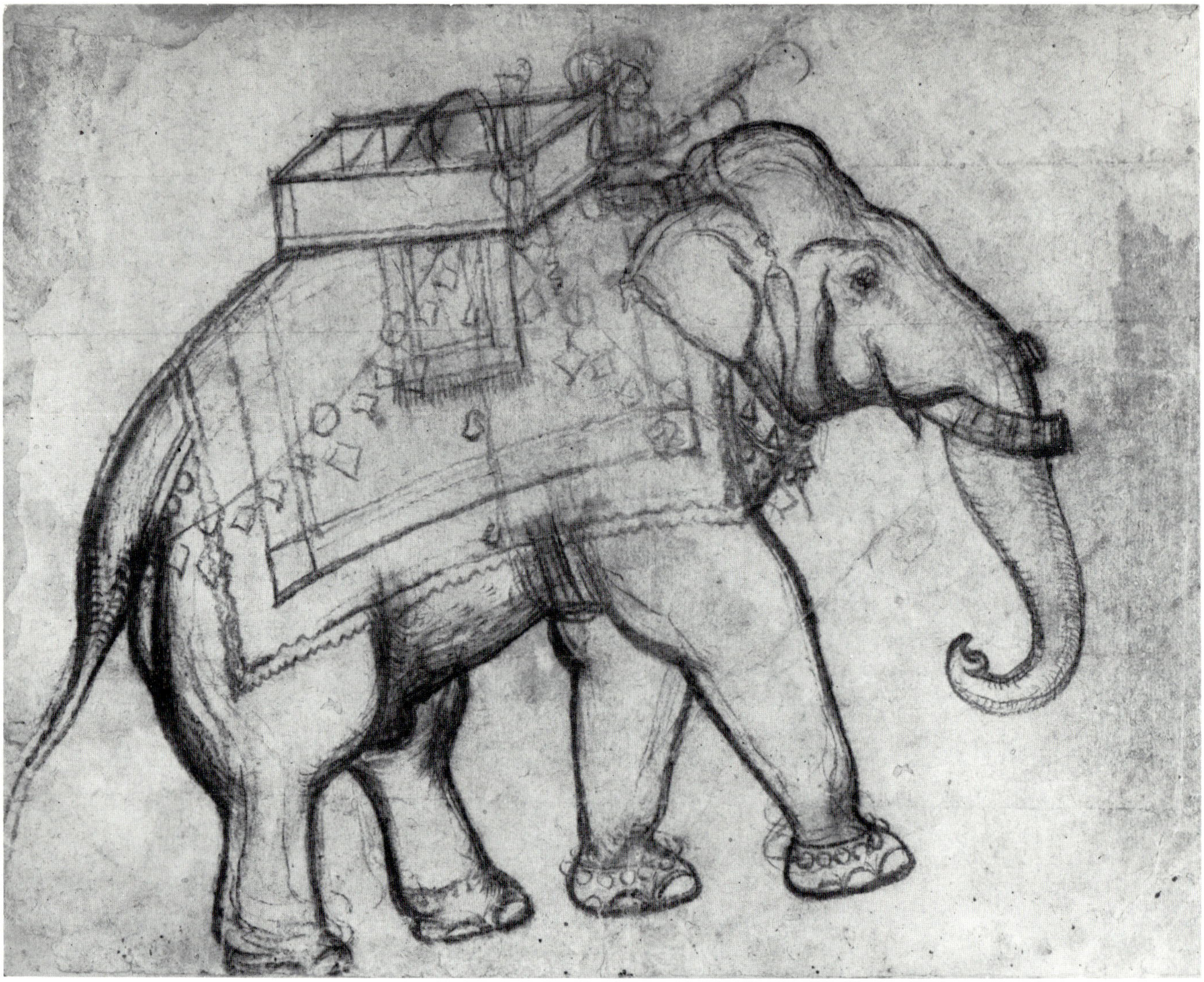

28 **Elephant with howdah**

Rajasthan, Kotah, early eighteenth century
Charcoal drawing 406 × 508 mm
Private collection

In spite of the looseness of execution, this is probably not drawn from life. More likely it is an under-drawing, which would then be over-painted in black with the point of a brush and the charcoal then finally erased. HH

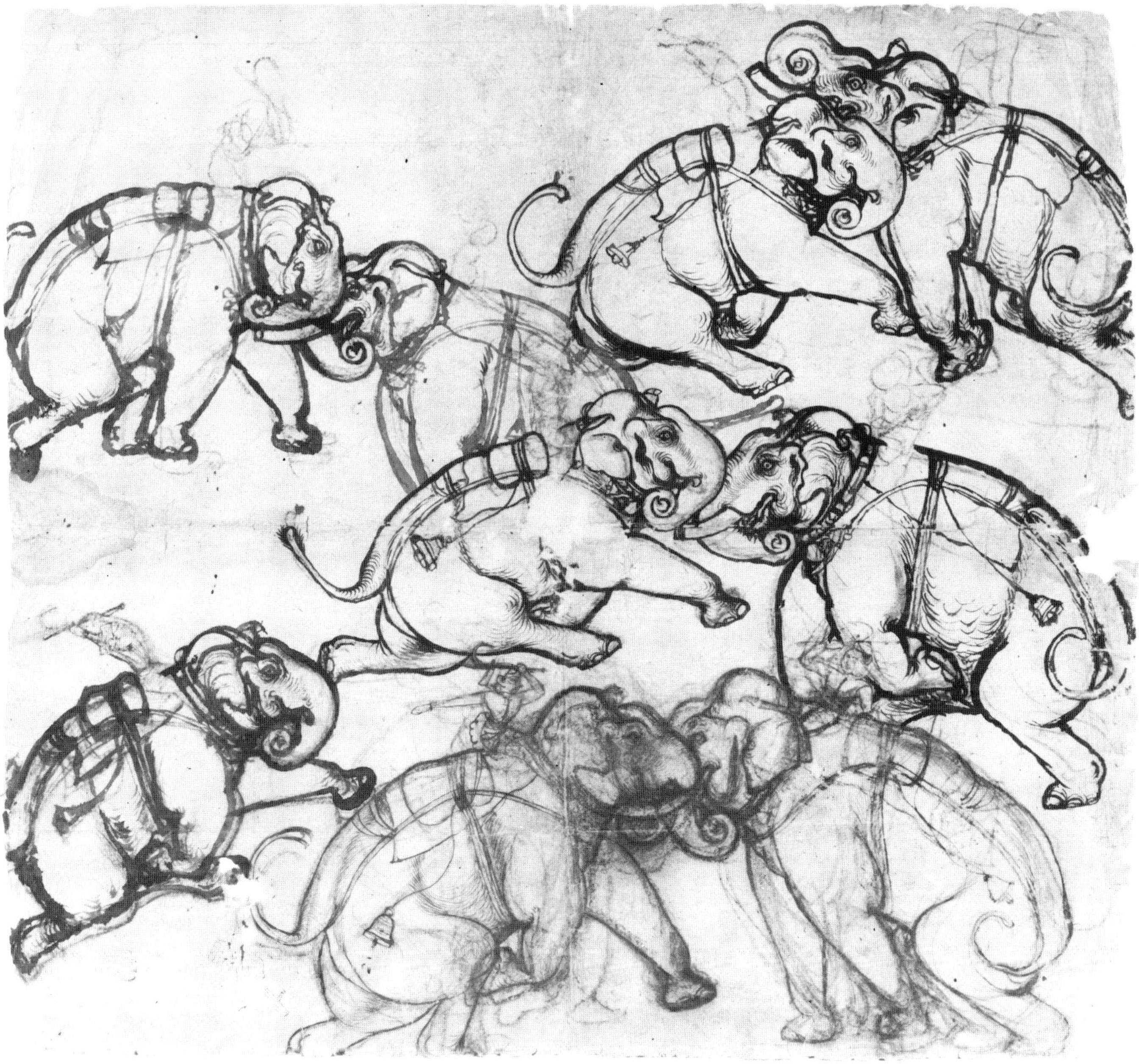

29 **Elephant combat**

Rajasthan, Kotah, early eighteenth century
Brush and charcoal drawing on paper 512 × 565 mm
Private collection

This extraordinary page of action studies begun in charcoal and then finally gone over with brush and ink, shows us the first stage of the process by which a great Kotah artist worked towards his final design. Studies such as this, must have been made in preparation for drawings like no. 23 and no. 26. HH

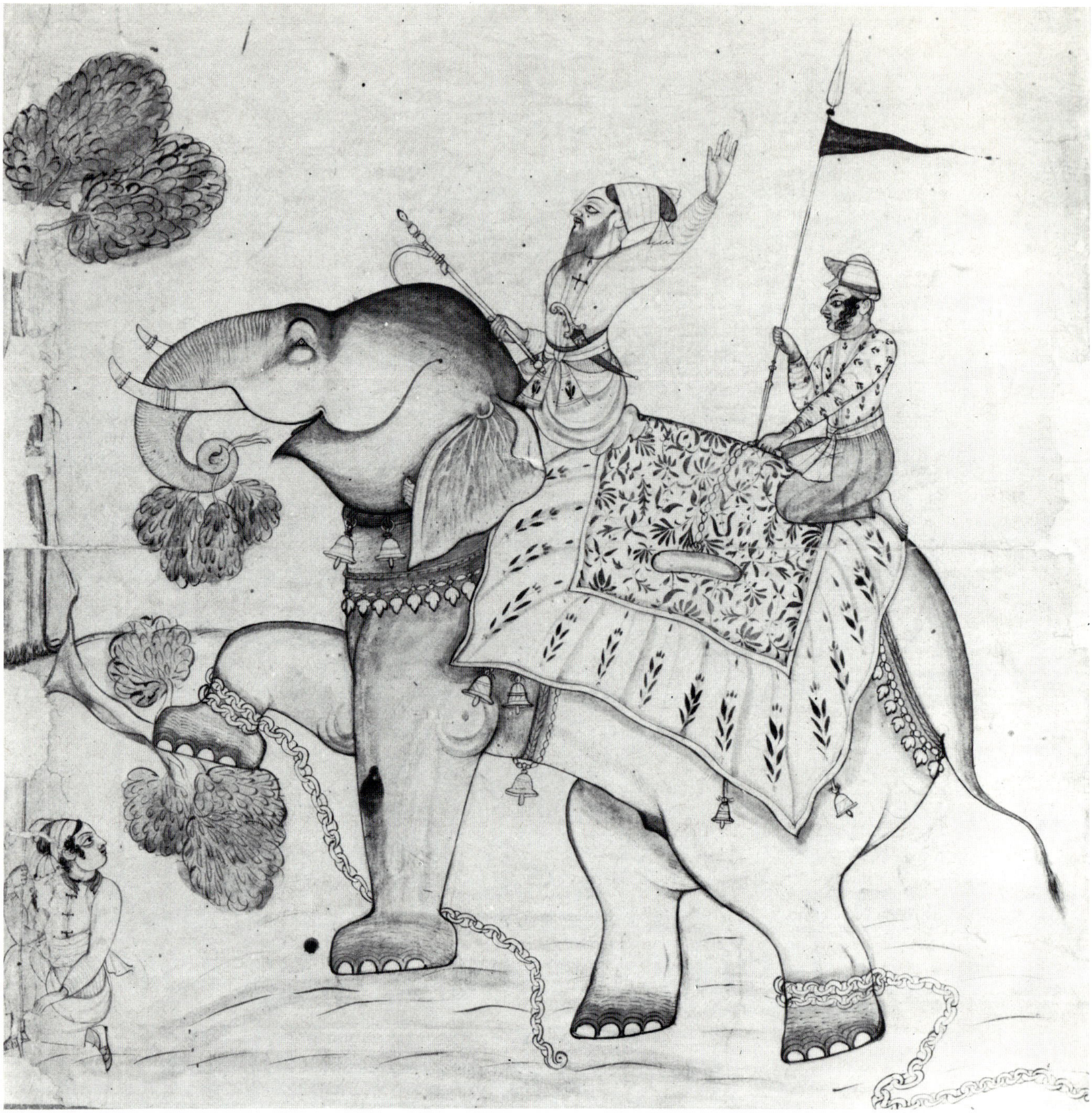

30 **An elephant eating a tree**
Punjab Hills, probably Mankot, *c* 1700
Brush drawing on paper with slight colour 368 × 381 mm
Private collection

The grand almost hieratic design is typical of Hill painting at this date. Certain details such as the drawing of the feet, suggest that the artist had never actually seen an elephant. HH

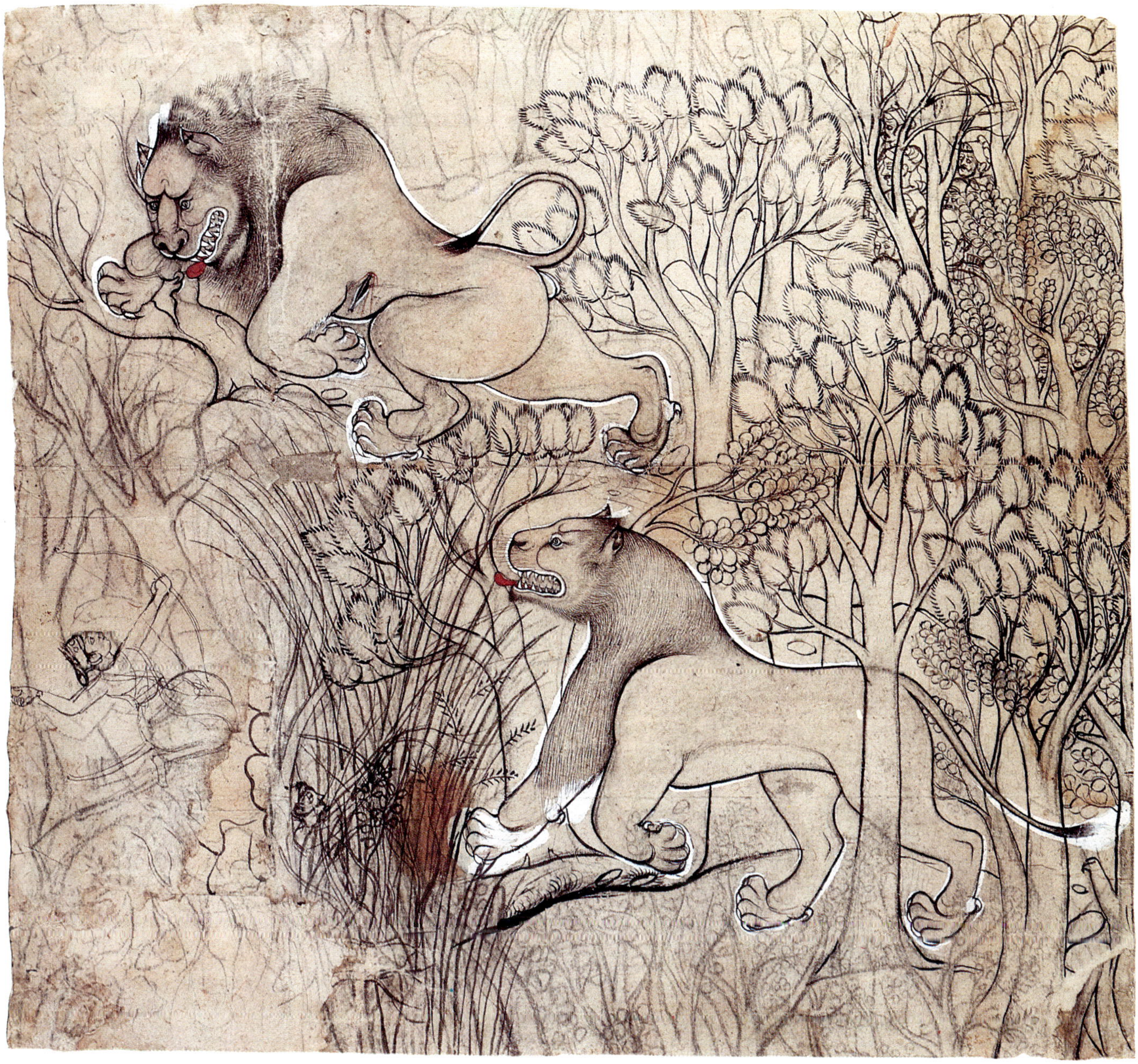

31 Lion hunt

Rajasthan, Kotah, *c* 1745
Brush drawing with colour 496 × 535 mm
Literature: S. C. Welch, 1976, no. 53
Private collection

This drawing is related to a painting of virtually identical composition, but with the addition of figures (See M. C. Beach, 1974, fig. 86. pl. LXXXI). The status of the drawing and the painting in relation to each other is difficult to determine. The energy and decision which we find here, seems to some extent lacking in the painting. Professor Welch suggests that the painting antedates the drawing, but it is of such quality that it is hard to believe that it is a later version. HH

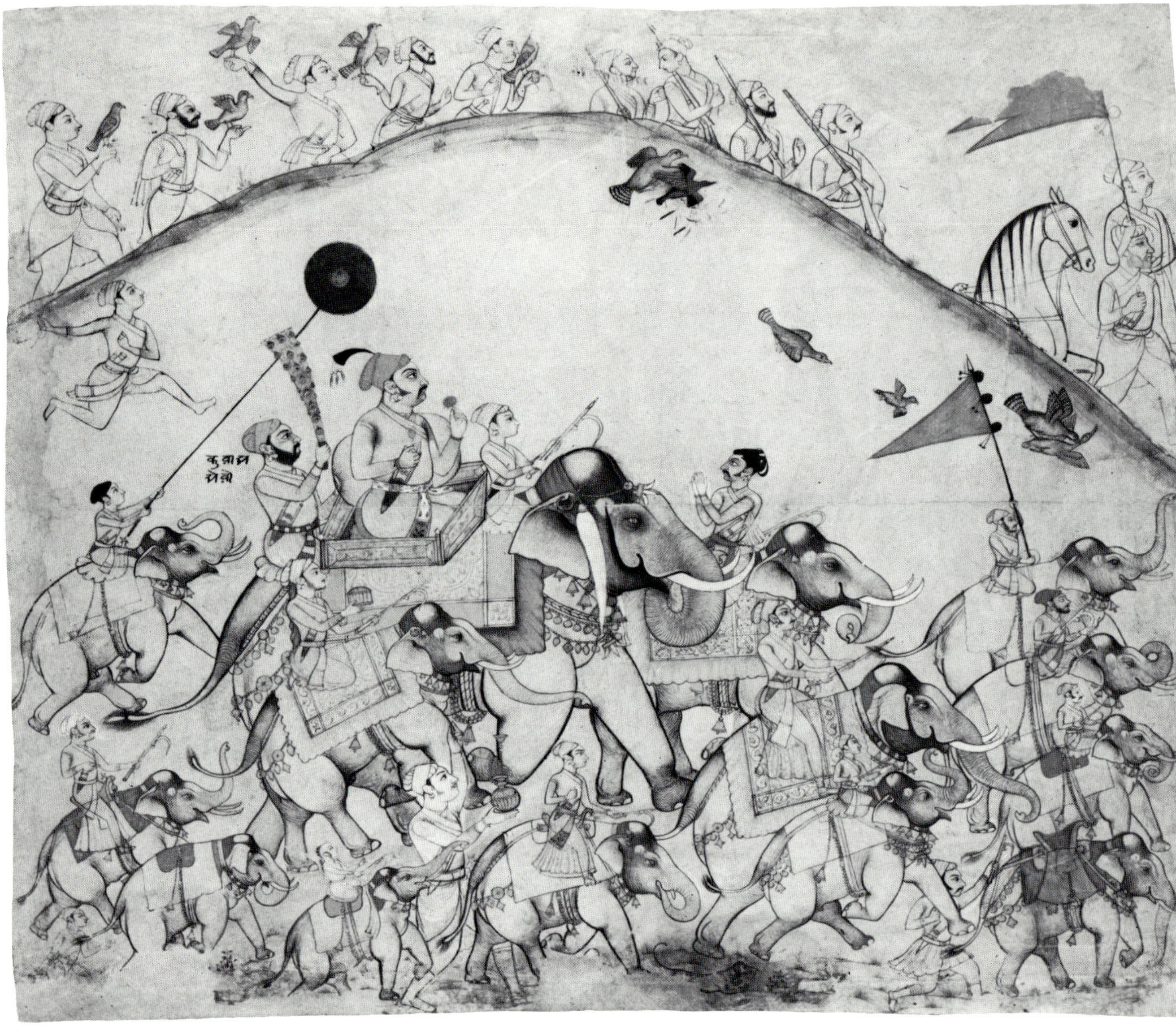

32 Hunting scene with fourteen elephants

Rajasthan, Sawar, early eighteenth century

Brush and black ink, heightened with colour and touches of white, on paper 521 × 610 mm

Inscribed on the reverse with the name of the patron: '*Maharaj sri rajai Singhji*', or '*Maharaja Jai Singh*', and dated 1656 (samvat 1713)

Private collection

Sawar is a *thikana* (feudatory) of the Ajmer district in Rajasthan. It was formed in the early seventeenth century under a grant from the Emperor Jahangir.

The technical elaboration of the drawing itself suggests that it must have been made as a work of art in its own right rather than as a study for something else.

For other drawings of Jai Singh see no. 42 and S. Lee. 1960, no. 52.

HH

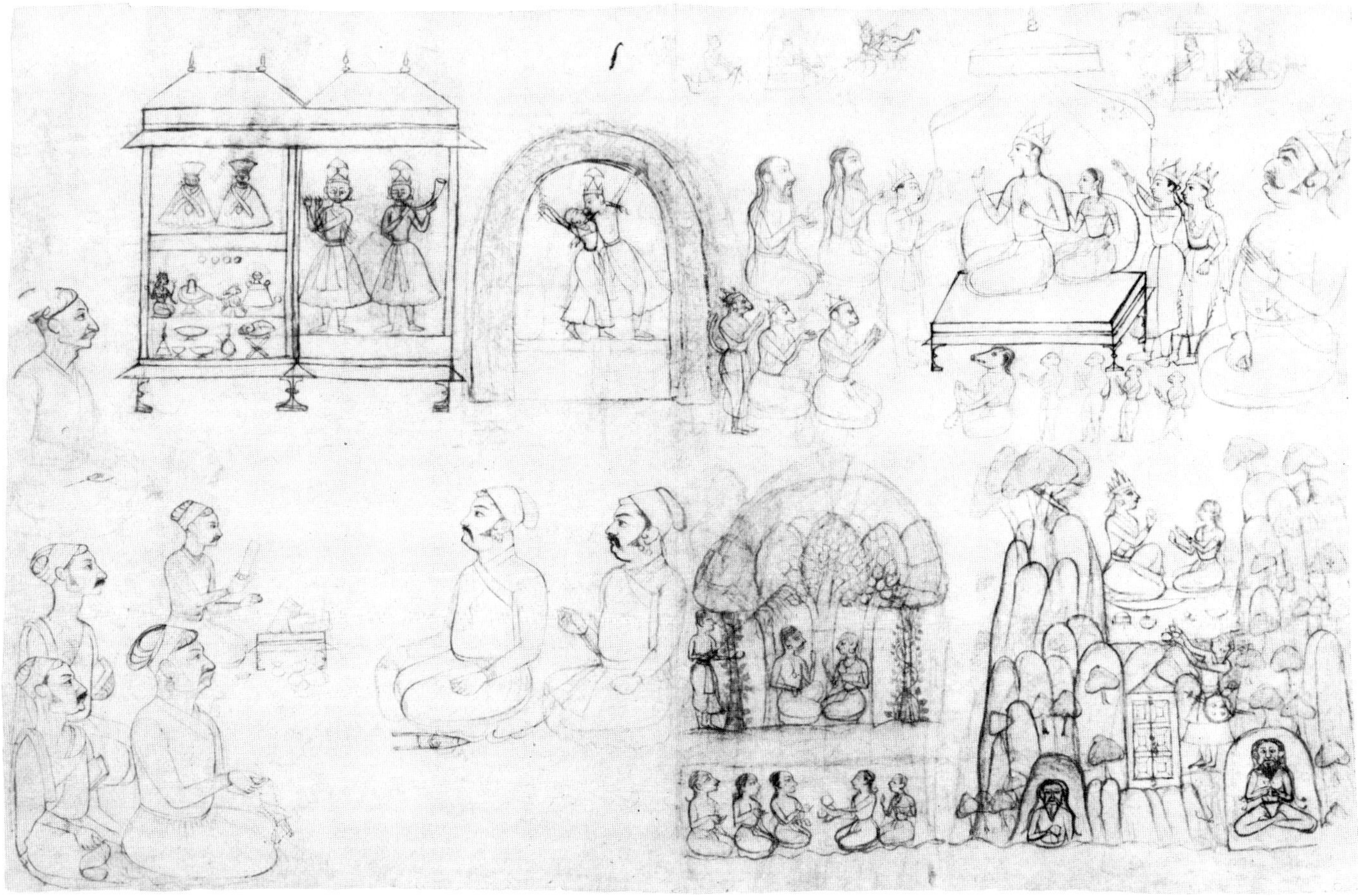

33 Page of sketches
Rajasthan, Sawar, *c* 1700
Brush drawing 406 × 629 mm
Private collection

A random collection of figure studies and designs for pictures, apparently by the same hand as no. 32 in which the heads of some of the figures in the bottom left hand corner re-appear. HH

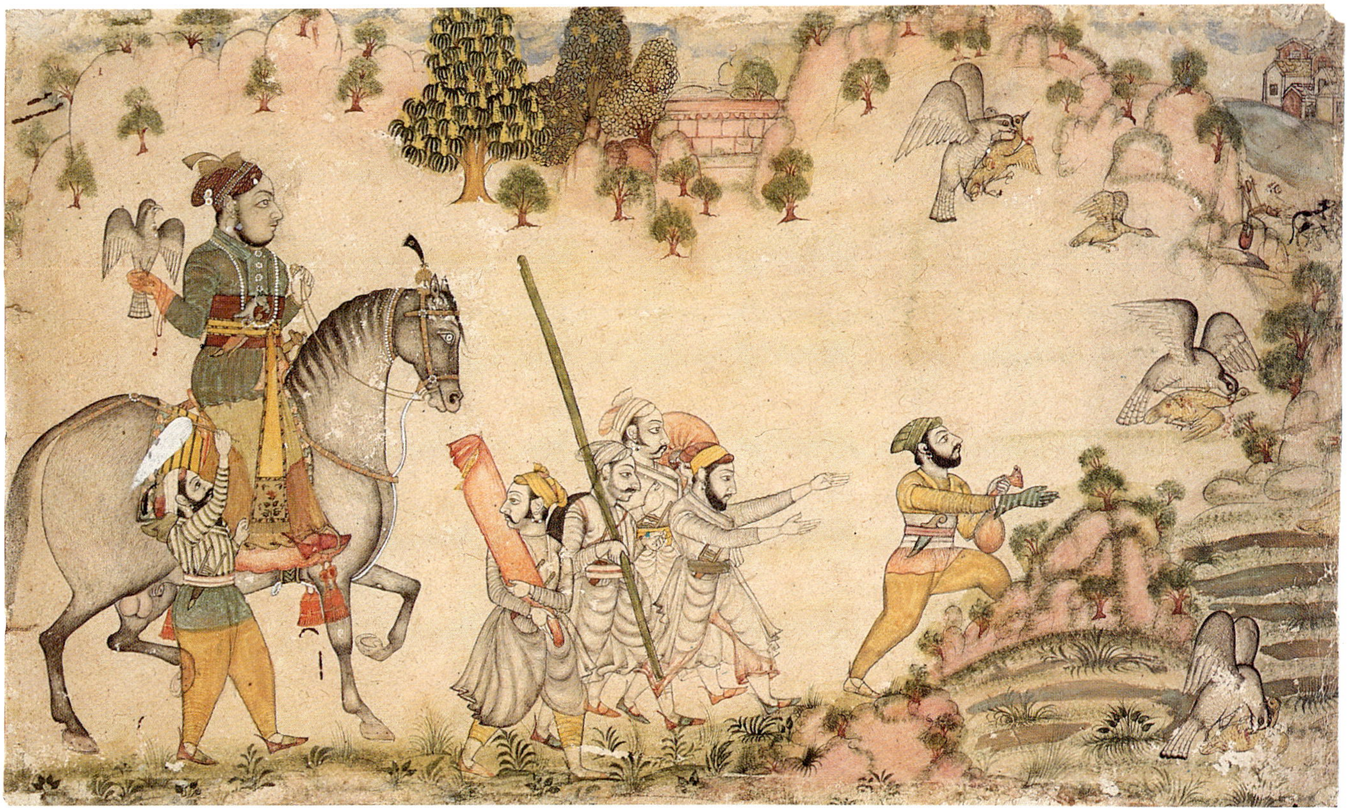

34 Thakur Sangram Singh Ranawat on horseback
Rajasthan, Mewar, early eighteenth century
Brush and ink, heightened with colours and gold, on paper
310 × 435 mm
Private collection

The unusual heavily shaded technique, with slight colour, is typical of a small group of drawings made at Mewar in the late seventeenth and early eighteenth centuries. This is a particularly good example. Note the almost Romanesque group of attendants in the centre. HH

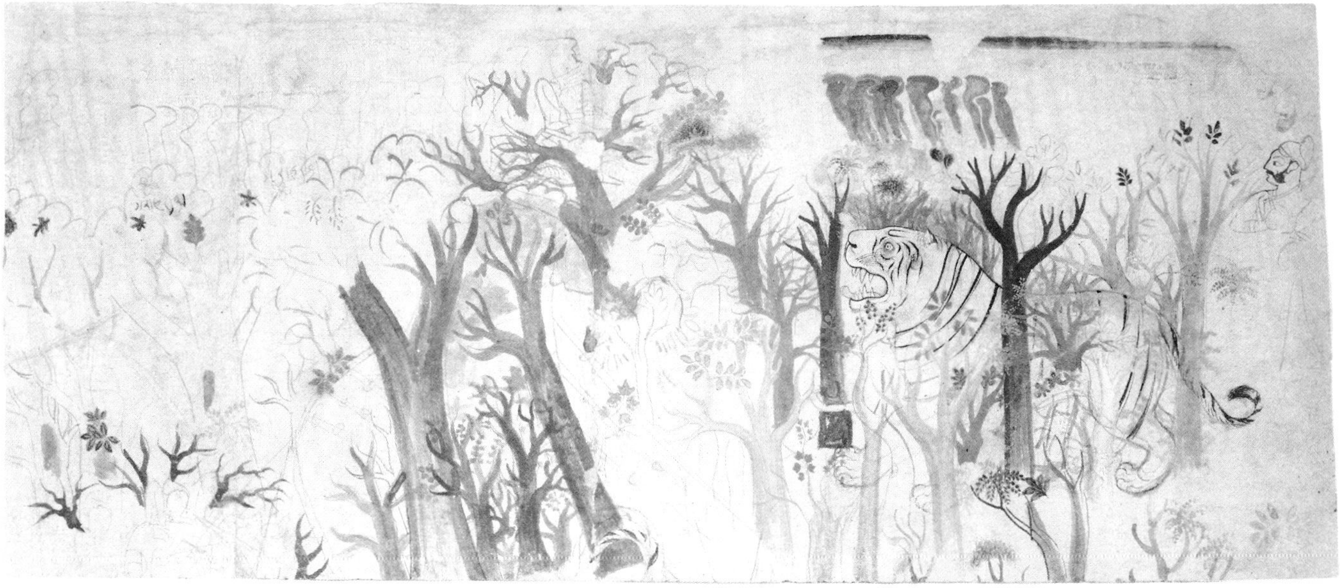

35 **Tiger hunt**
Rajasthan, Kotah School, dated 1780
Drawing in brush and grey ink, heightened with broad areas of colour, on paper (missing edges repaired)
With a four line inscription and other notations in *nagari* characters
300 × 720 mm
Private collection

This unfinished painting was probably twice as large before it was trimmed along the line now forming the lower margin. This loss is unfortunate, but it has not affected or diminished the ecstatic qualities of the surviving work. Maharao Umed Singh of Kotah (*c* 1770–1819) is taking aim from a shooting platform in the tree at top centre. His two colleagues are protected in a safe perch at the lower left. Various attendants stand along the right margin, at some distance from the giant tiger, that commands the scene like some primal force. The expressionistic qualities of this work are only in part the result of personal temperament. They also derive from the excited rhythms of untrammelled thought. This is a work in progress, arrested at a vital stage. Note the urgent patches and blobs – colour notations really – and the feverish, entangled lines that have only begun to unfold. TM

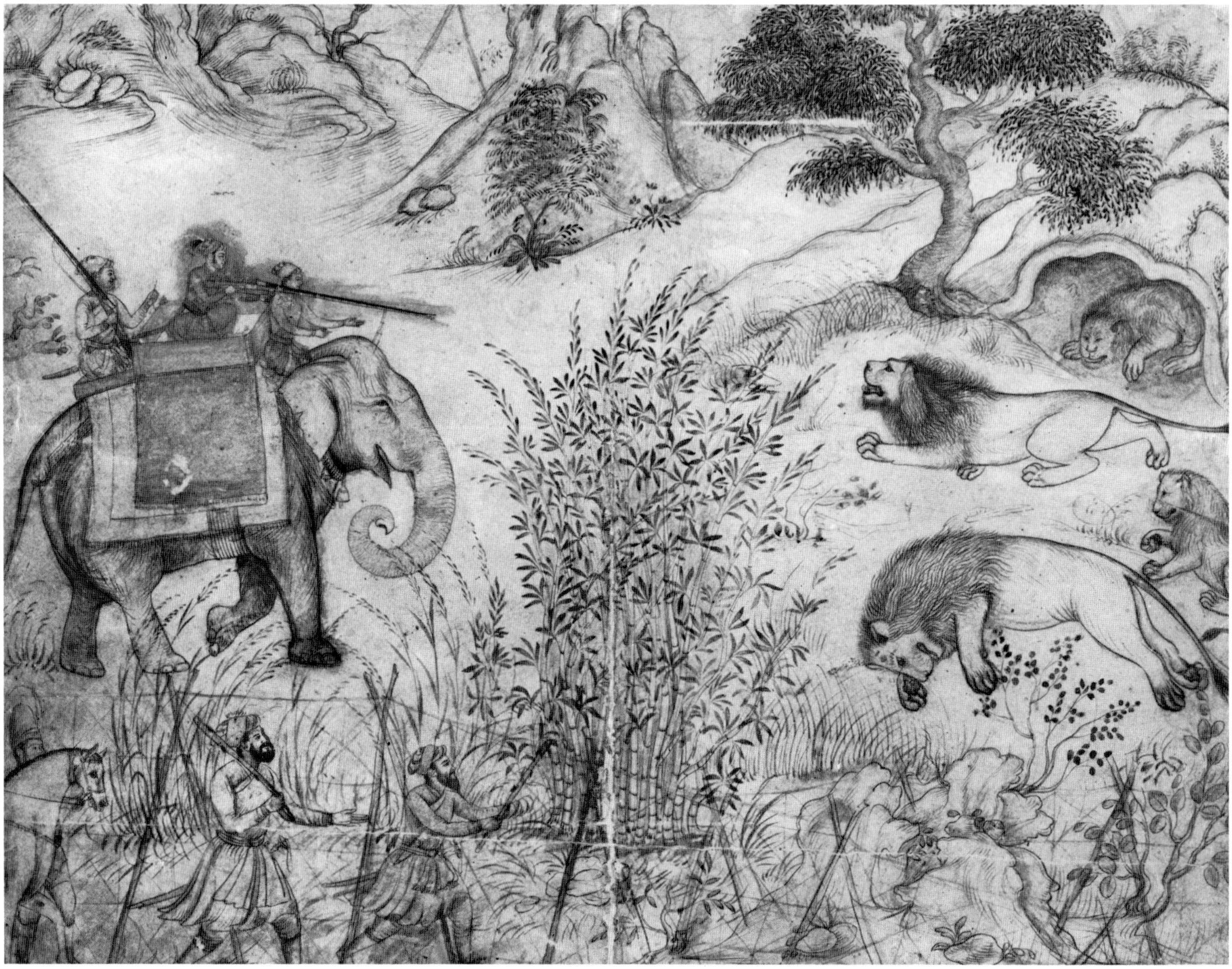

36 **A Royal lion hunt**
Mughal, *c* 1660
Brush and ink, heightened with colour, on paper 273 × 356 mm
Private collection

A compositional study, somewhat trimmed, for a major Mughal painting. TM

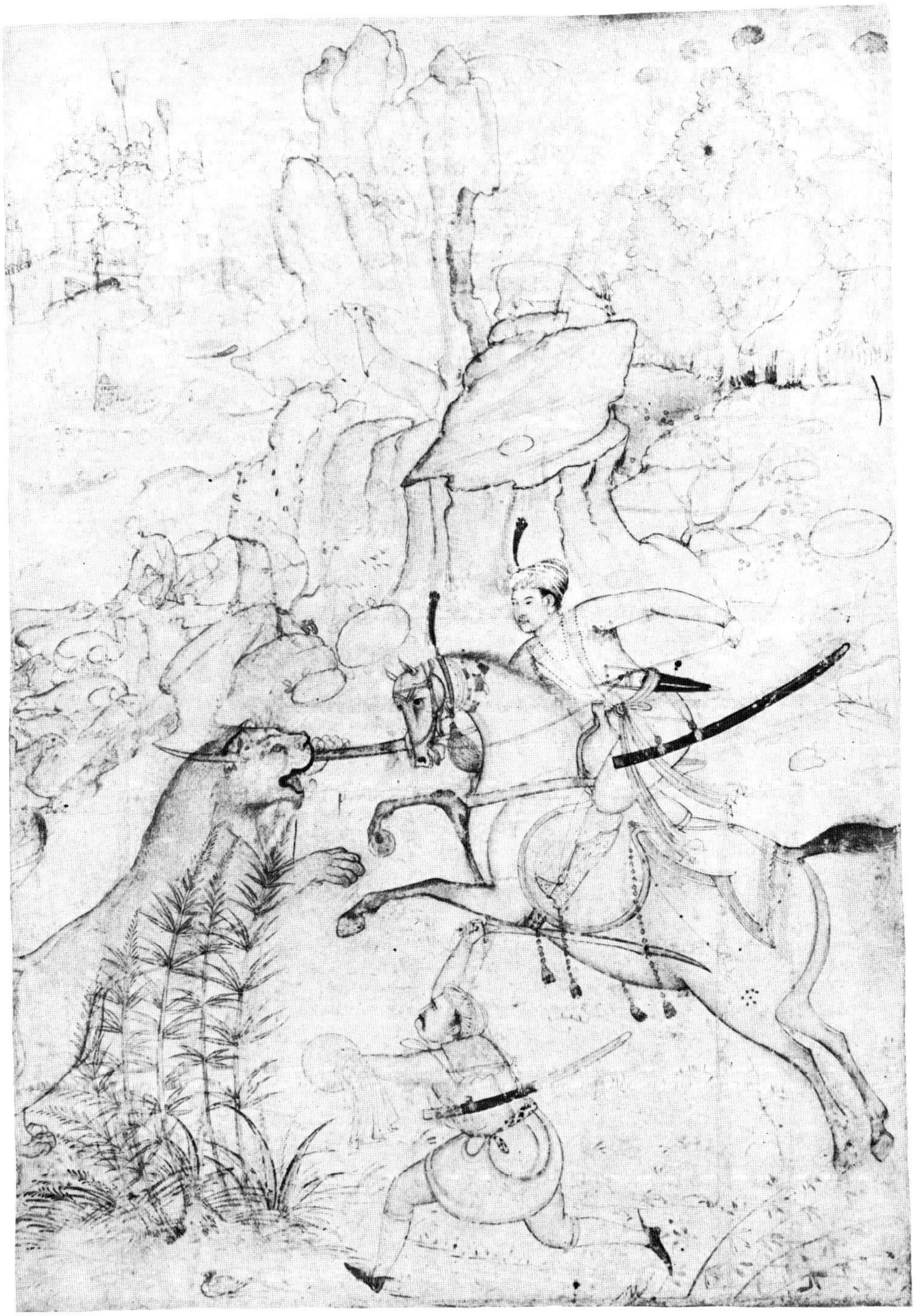

37 A prince on horseback slaying a lion

Mughal, *c* 1600

Drawing in brush and black ink, heightened with touches of gold and colour, on white-primed paper

With dark blue margins of a later date, decorated with floral arabesques in gold; mounted on a card 240 × 166 mm; page 327 × 223 mm

Catherine and Ralph Benkaim Collection

This work is actually the underdrawing for an ambitious miniature that was never completed beyond an initial flourish of colour, although its surface has been made ready for paint. (Note the white priming overall.) The hunt scene format, with the principle figures looming large in the foreground and a deep landscape receding in staggered layers beyond, was the preferred composition during the 'heroic' period of Mughal painting, at the time of Akbar the Great (r. 1556–1605). TM

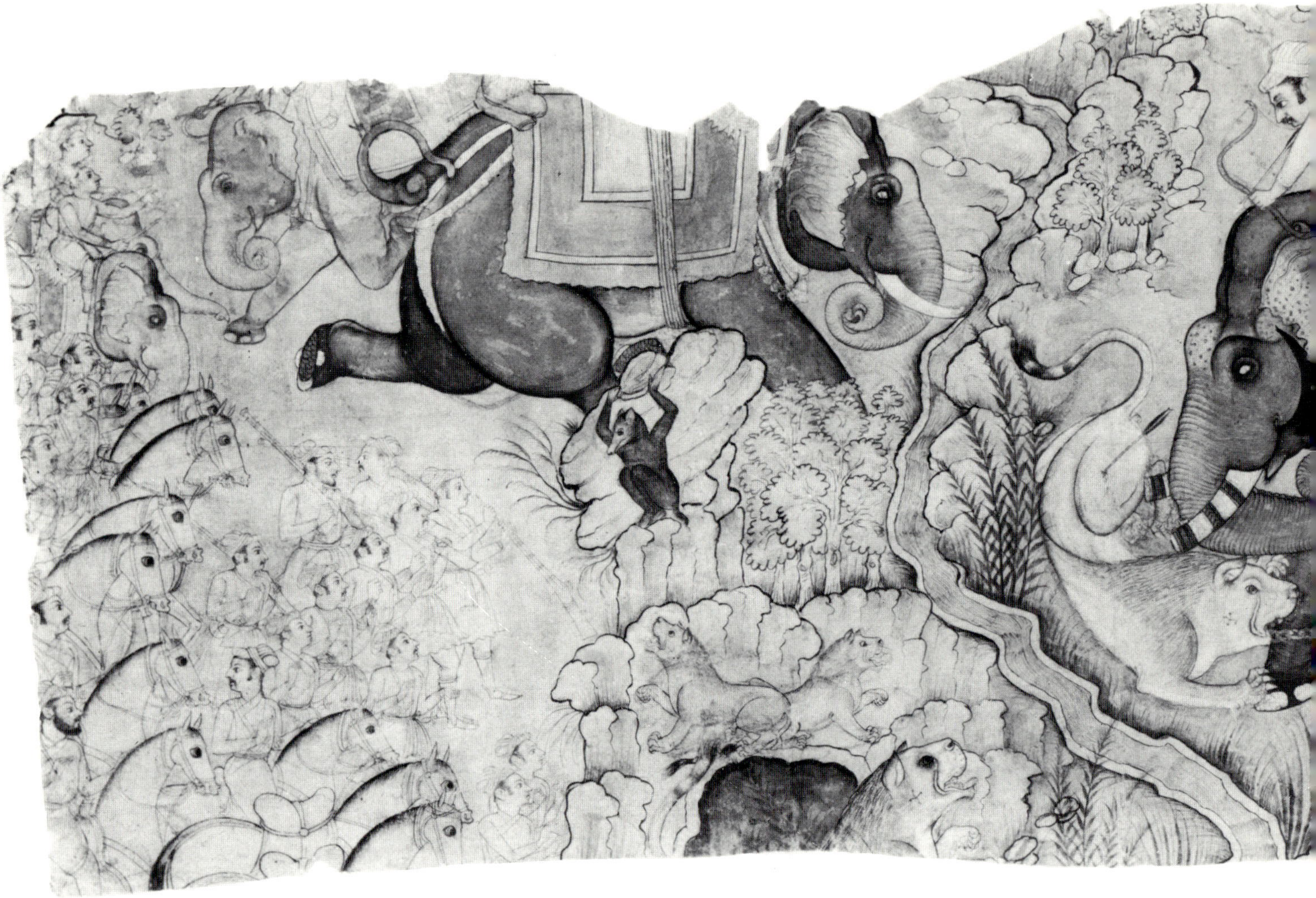

38 **A royal elephant hunt**
Rajasthan, *c* 1630
Brush and ink on paper 362 × 1074 mm
Private collection

Though only a fragment, what remains is probably the central core of an exceptionally large and splendid drawing. It owes much to earlier Mughal hunting scenes, but these were executed on a minute scale and in a far more refined technique. There is a boldness of invention and confident use of scale peculiar to the Rajput tradition of drawing. But as yet, both the identity of the ruler shooting the lion, and the place where the drawing was made, are yet unknown. HH

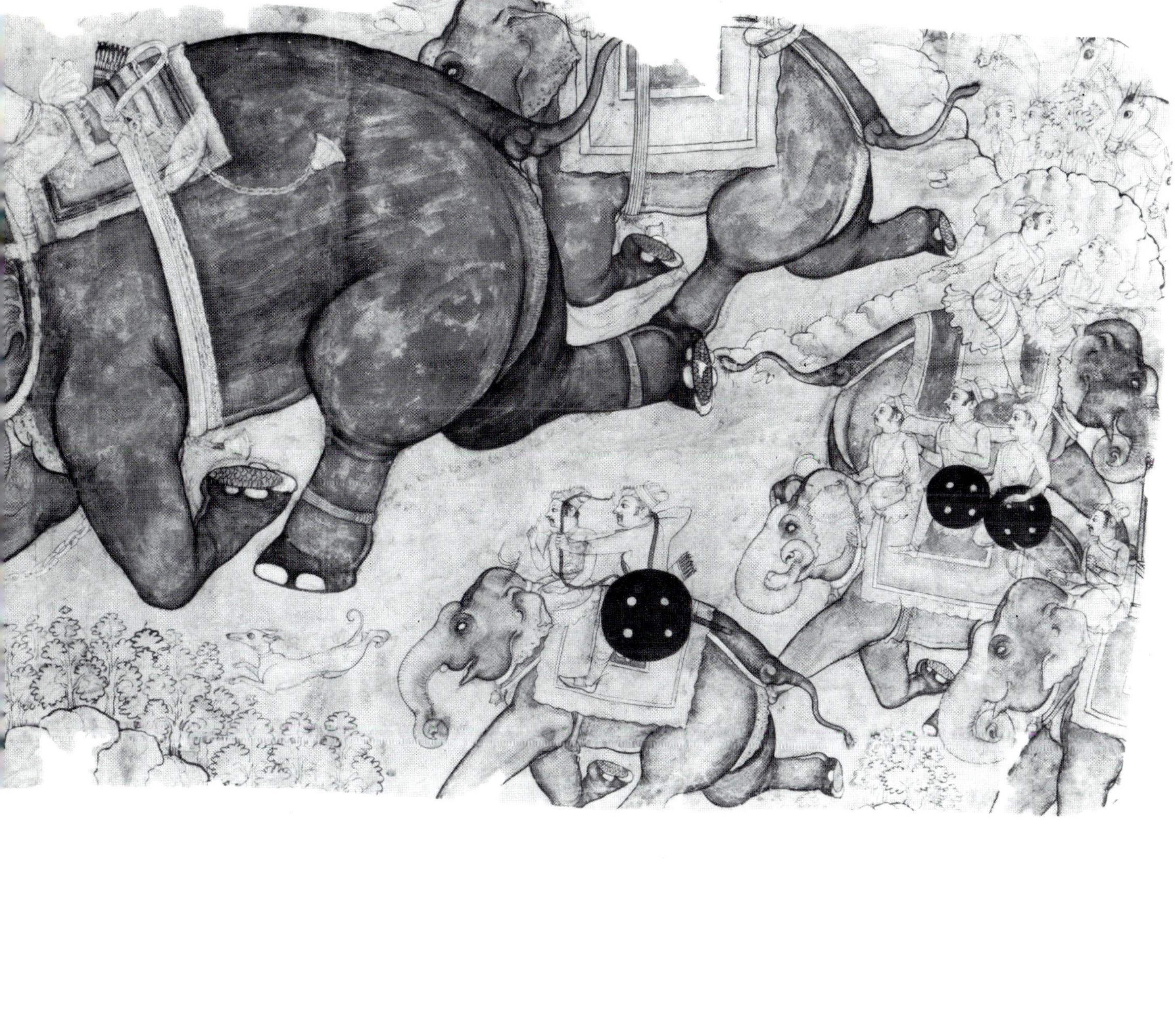

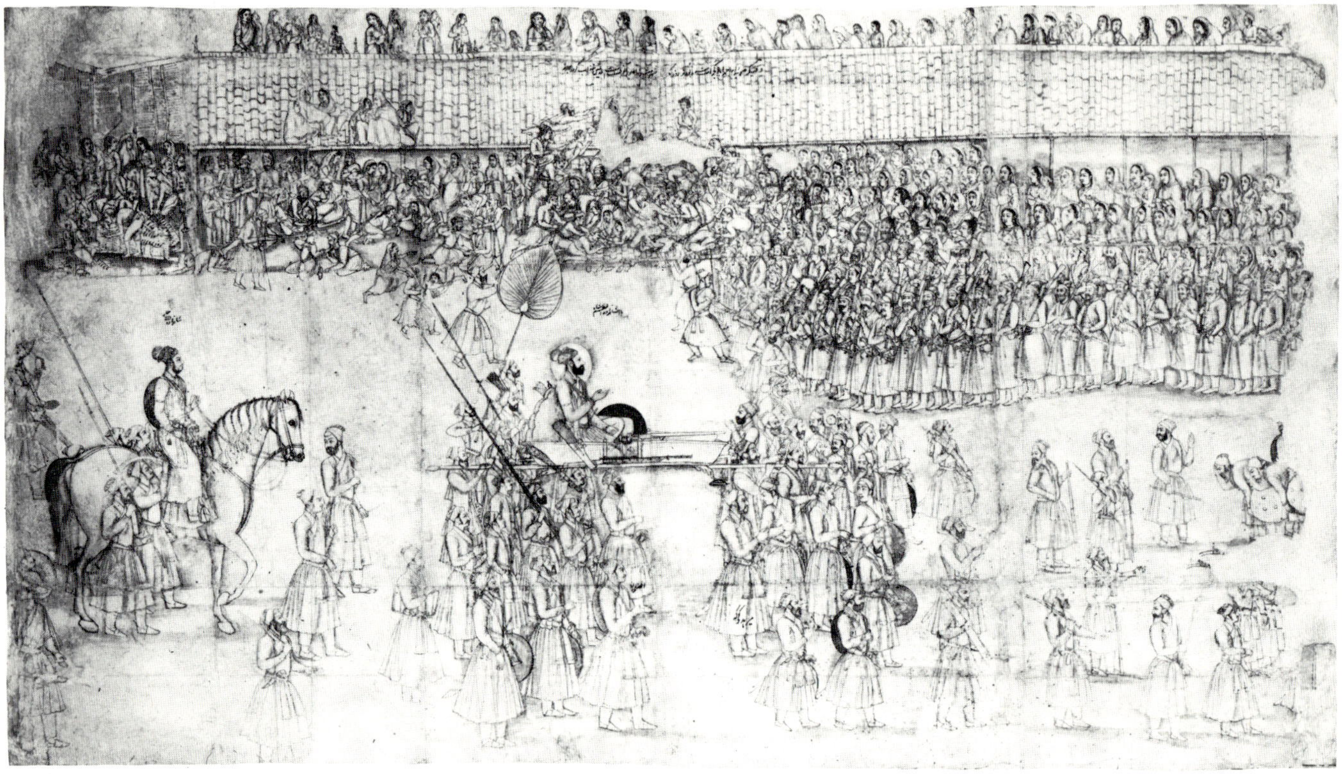

39 **Prince Azam Shah enters Ahmedabad**
Mughal, *c* 1701
Brush and black ink, heightened with gold and touches of colour, on paper 483 × 711 mm
Inscribed: *Prince Azam Shah / Exalted Prince / When he became Governor of Ahmedabad in Gujerat, he entered the city. This is a picture of that time. They had* . . . (word illegible)
Literature: S. C. Welch, 1976, no. 22
Private collection

This drawing shows the formal entry of Prince Azam Shah into the city of Ahmedabad when he was made Governor of Gujerat in 1701 and it was presumably made to commemorate the occasion. The detail is almost photographic and many of the faces in the crowd appear to be portraits. If one looks hard enough, one can find the head of a negro in the large group on the right. In the centre, people scramble for gold coins distributed as part of the celebrations. HH

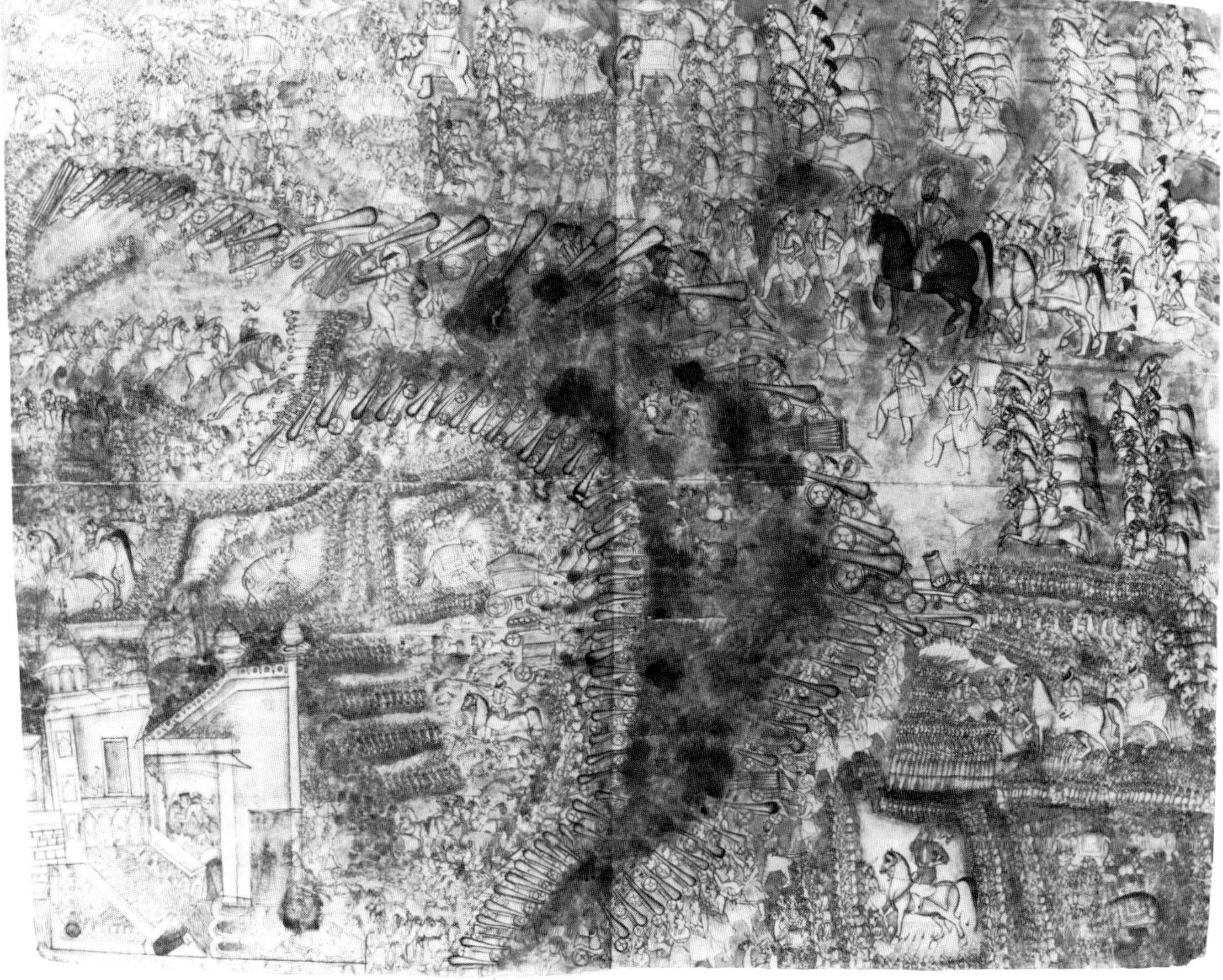

40 The battle of Panipat, 13 January 1761

Mughal, Faizabad, *c* 1770
Johnson Album 66, no. 3
Drawing with some colour, on paper backed with cloth, through which can be seen a drawing of a horseman and attendant
510 × 660 mm
Inscribed with the names of the principal combatants in Persian characters
Literature: T. Falk and M. Archer, 1981, p. 150
British Library, India Office Library and Records

'Ahmad Shah Durrani and his forces are defeating Shadashiva Bhao and the Maratha armies: Ahmad Shah Durrani rides a brown stallion surrounded by his close supporters. On his left are Najib Khan and Shuja ud-Daula with their forces, on his right are Ahmad Khan Bangash and Hafiz Rahmat, before them a cavalry attack is made by Shah Wali Khan. Within the buildings of the Panipar camp troops are raping and committing atrocities while outside the wounded Bhao is helped from his horse: the centre of the picture is dominated by the arc of the two lines of guns with smoke and devastation between them.' (op. cit.)

This is a later and coarser panoramic view than no. 39. HH

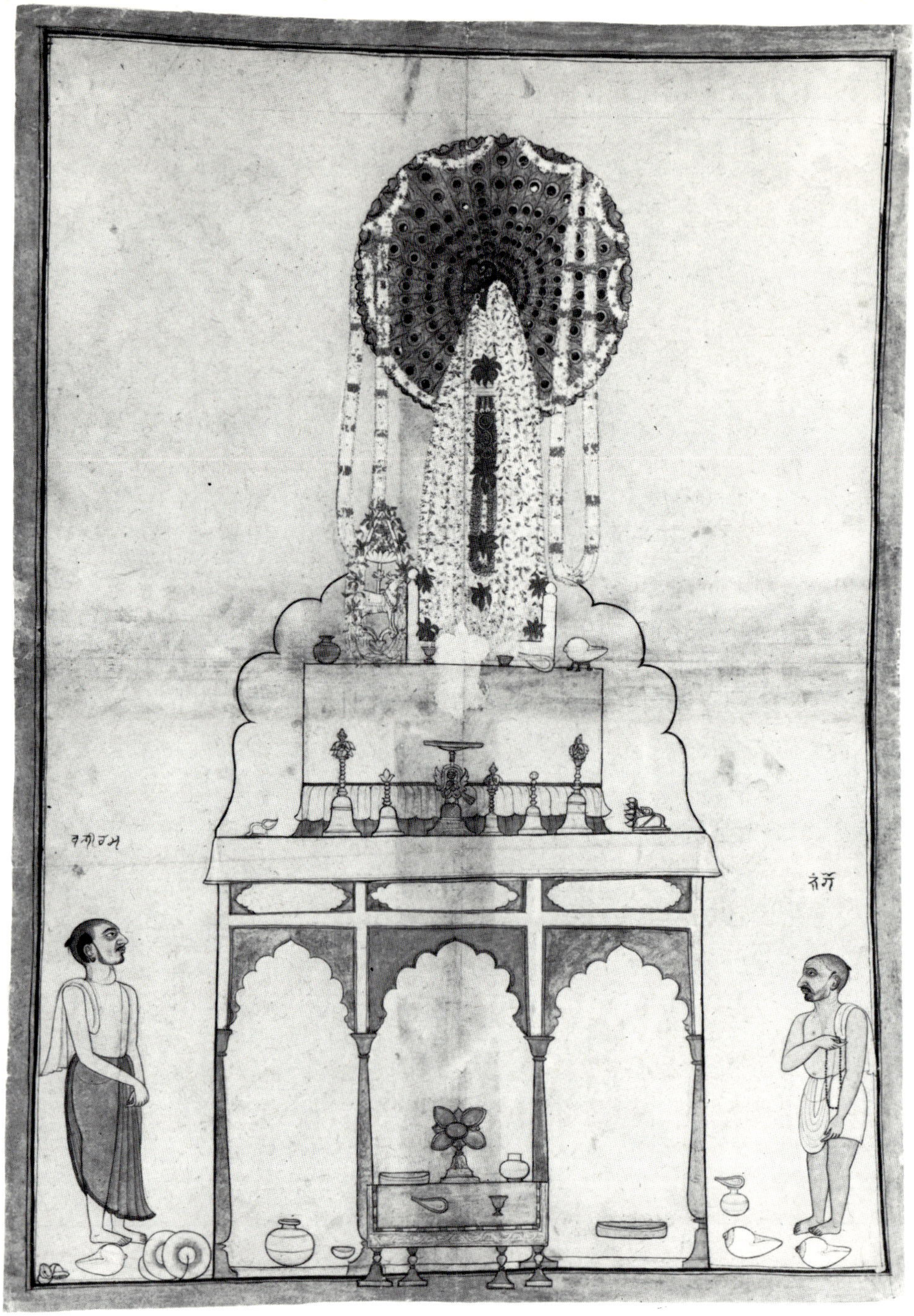

41 **Two devotees in attendance upon a double Krishna shrine draped with garlands**

Punjab Hills, Chamba, *c* 1740

Brush drawing with slight colour 610 × 445 mm

Private collection

A remarkably formal drawing, thought to have been a study for a wall painting but the elaborate execution particularly noticeable in the peacock's tail and the garland, suggests it was made for its own sake.

HH

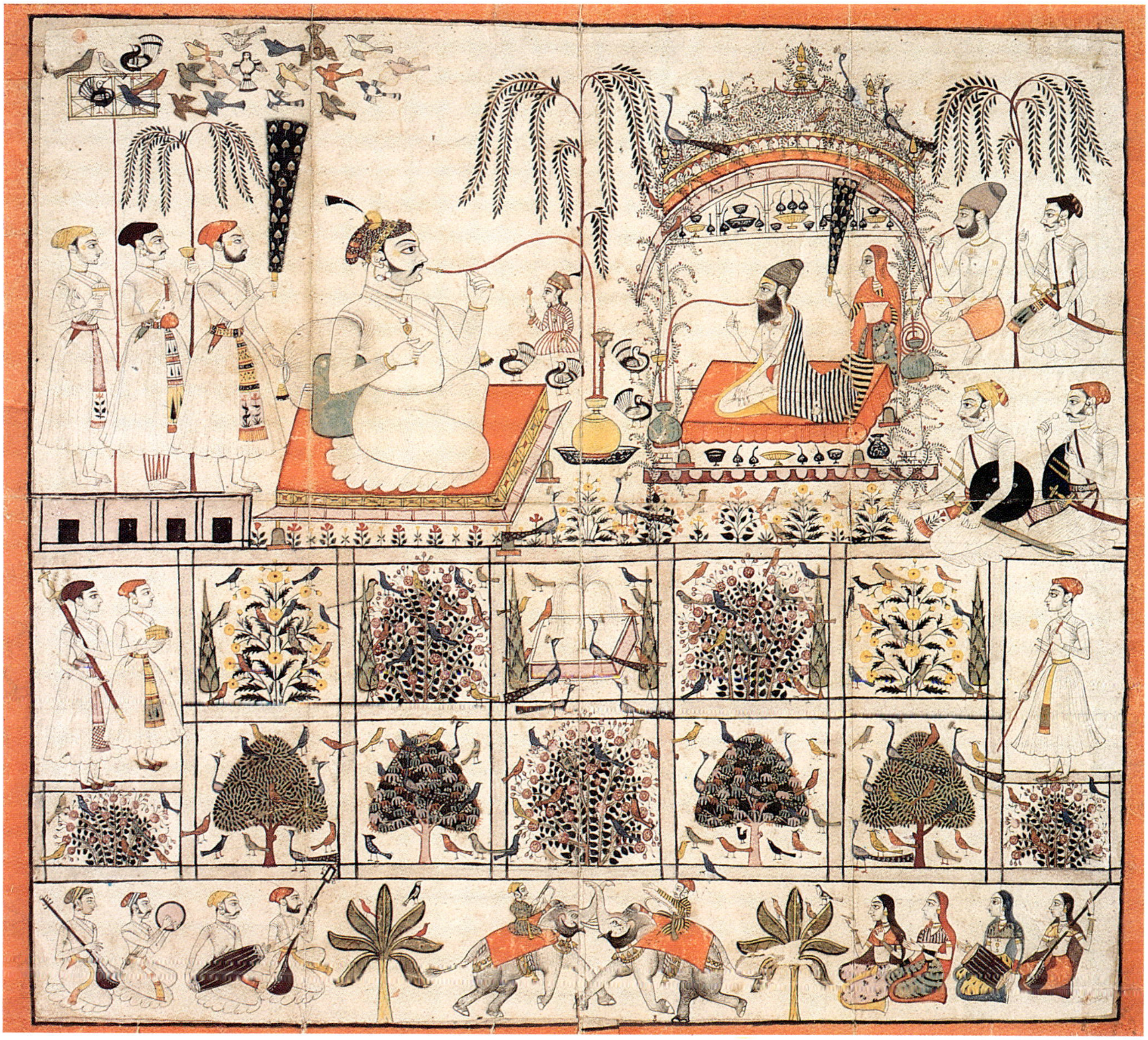

42 Raj Singh of Sawar visiting a yogi in a garden
Rajasthan, Sawar, 1714
Brush drawing, partially coloured 472 × 520 mm
Private collection

The purpose of a drawing such as this is obscure. Elaborate and brightly coloured without in any sense being a preparation for a painting, it must either have been commemorative, perhaps for presentation to the Ruler, or have been made as a maquette for a wall painting. It has a peculiar combination of the naive and sophisticated, particularly in terms of scale. One of the tame birds depicted in the top left hand corner shows a rare piece of foreshortening. HH

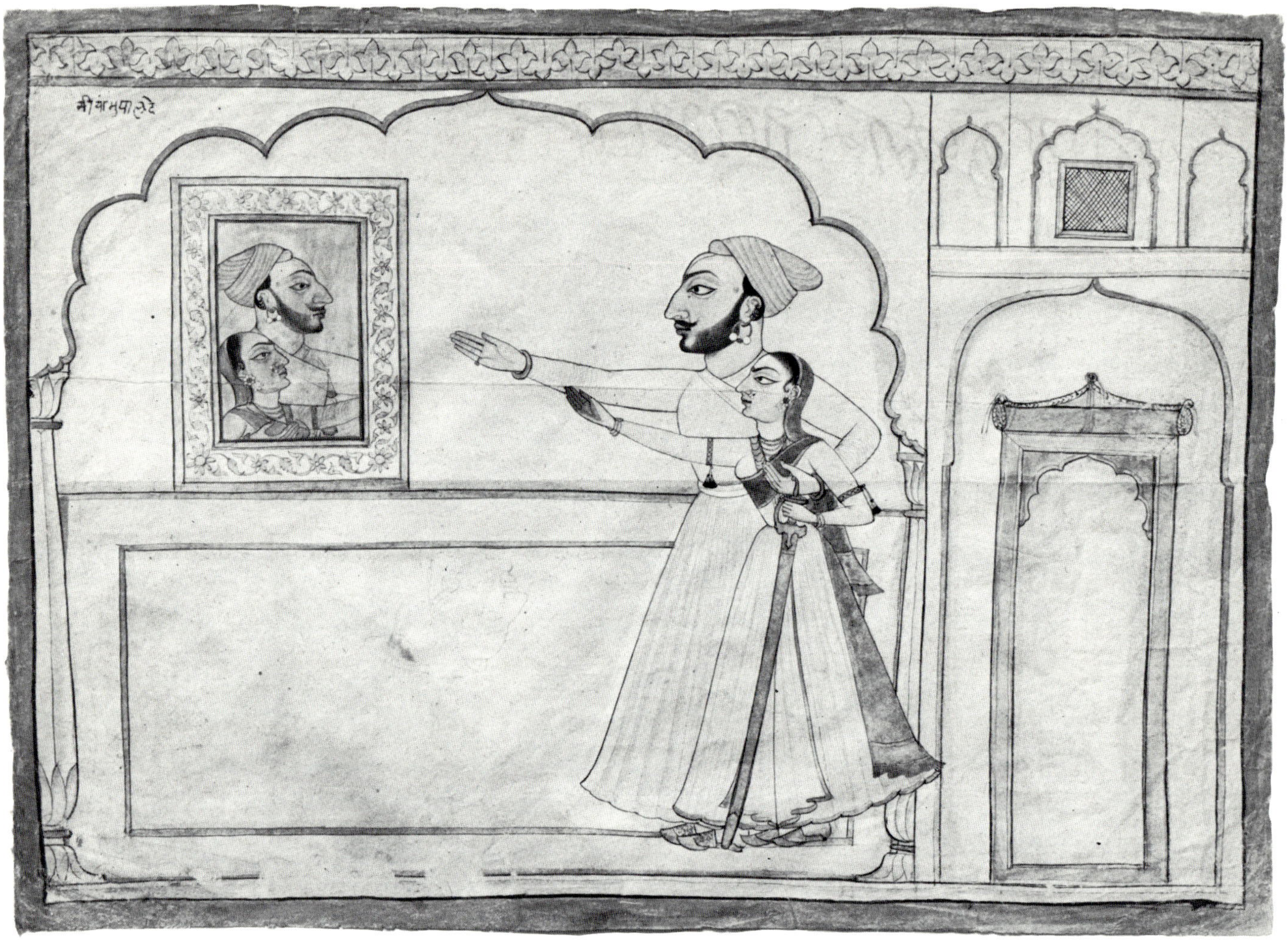

43 Prince Bhupal Dev of Jasrota, and a woman, reflected in a mirror

Punjab Hills, Chamba or Jasrota, *c* 1720

Drawing in brush and black ink, heightened with silver and colour washes, on light tan paper 222 × 312 mm

Inscribed in Takri on the verso: '*Prince Bhupal Dev of Jasrota*'

Catherine and Ralph Benkaim Collection

No other published portrait of Prince Bhupal Dev comes close to the panache or psychological acuity of this work. Bhupal Dev was obviously a man of considerable bravura, with unusual tastes: his portraitist would never have attempted this powerful image otherwise. For other portraits of Bhupal Dev, see W. G. Archer, 1973, vol. I, pp. 213–214; and C. A. Glynn, 1979, pp. 38–55. TM

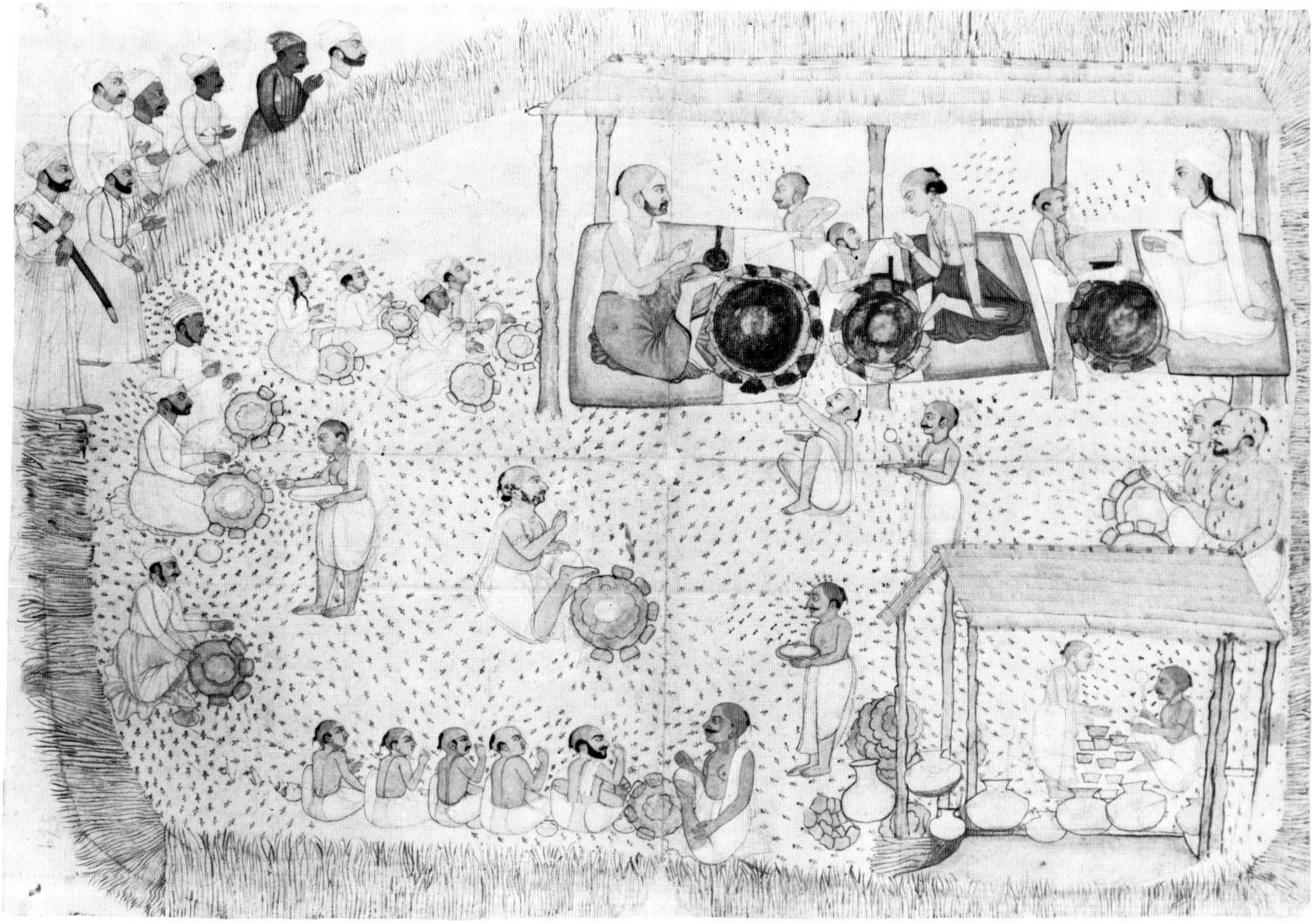

44 Factory at work (A meal in a stockade)
Punjab Hills, Chamba, *c* 1740
Brush and black ink, heightened with colour, on paper
410 × 590 mm
Literature: S. C. Welch, 1976, no. 75
Private collection

The subject of this drawing is so far unexplained. Many suggestions have been made, but none seem conclusive. Opinions even differ as to whether the drawing includes clouds of tiny insects or hundreds of minute blossoms. HH

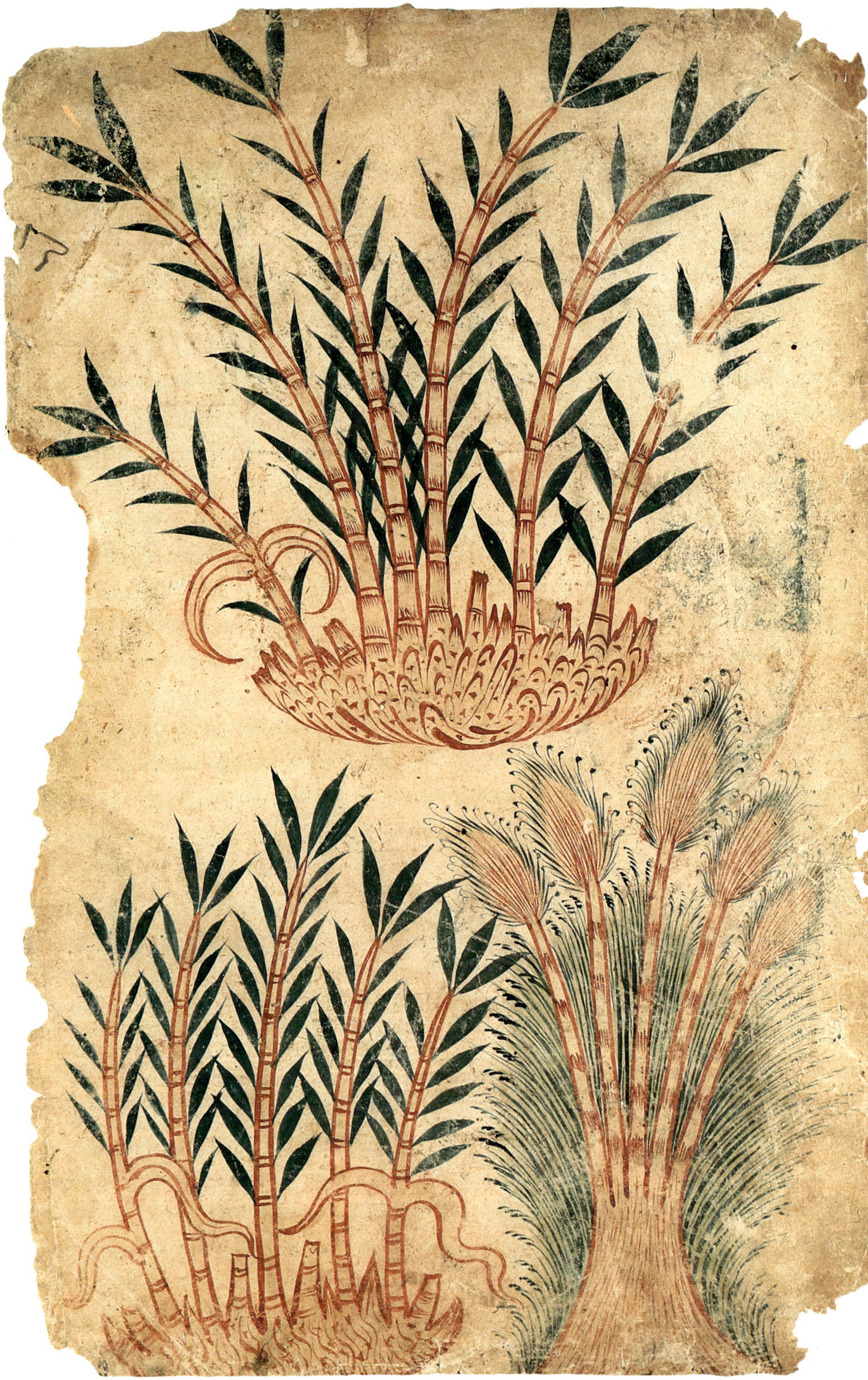

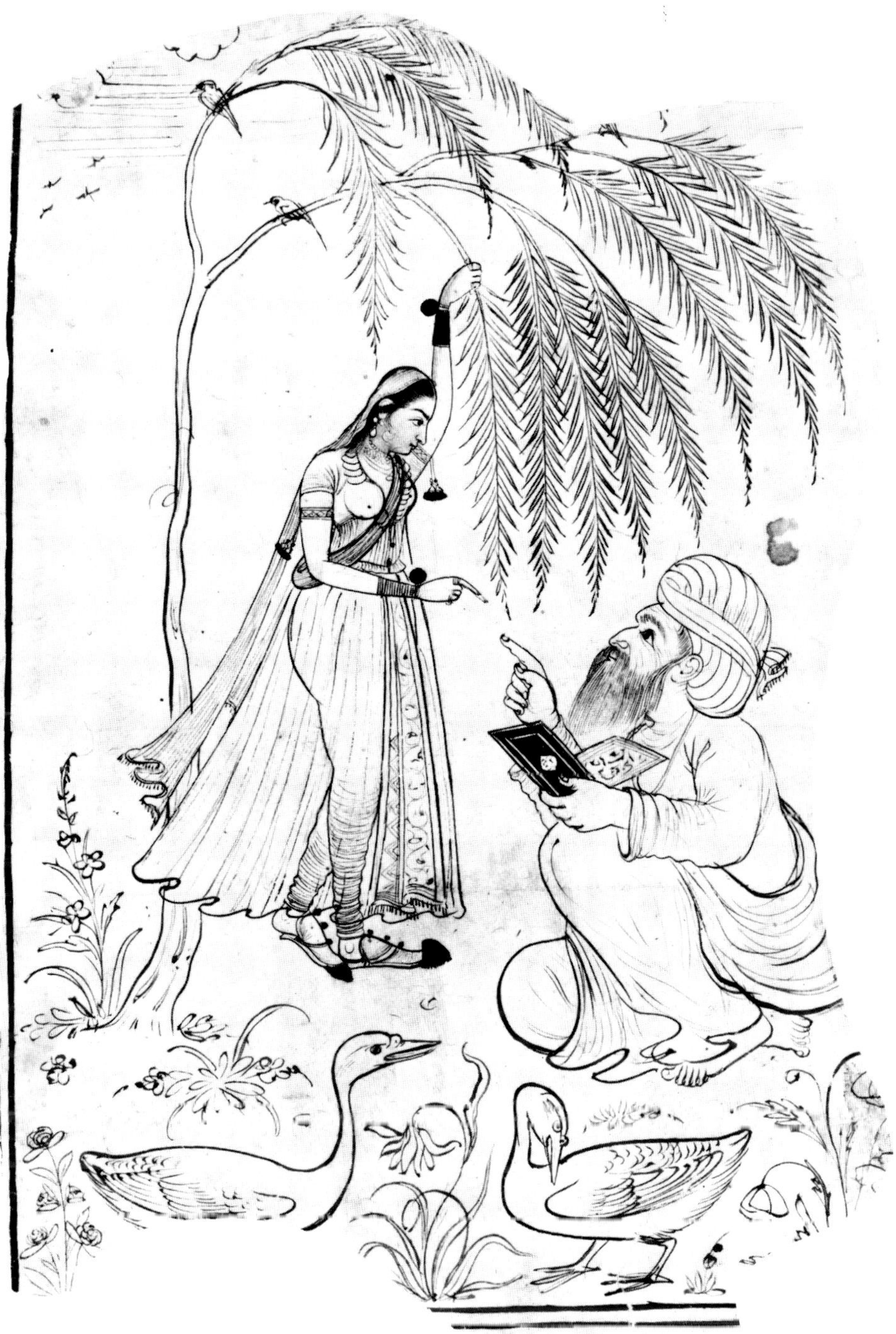

45 **Three Bamboo Plants**

Deccan, dated 1595
Brush and opaque watercolour, on paper 394 × 254 mm
Private collection

This is an illustration from an Indian copy of a celebrated Greek treatise, *De Materia Medica* by Pedacius Dioscorides, on the healing property of plants, dating originally from the first century AD.

Perhaps because the plant depicted is a bamboo and therefore familiar to the artist, he was inspired to make this memorable image, wholly Indian and yet curiously reminiscent of an ancient Egyptian wall painting.

Other folios from this manuscript have been published in T. McInerney, 1982, no. 17. HH

46 **Ajmer girl and holy man**

Rajasthan, Ajmer or Sarwar, *c* 1700
Brush drawing 263 × 173 mm
Private collection

This strange image to some extent reflects a seventeenth-century Persian prototype, though the girl herself and the tree under which she stands, are typical of Ajmer painting at this period. HH

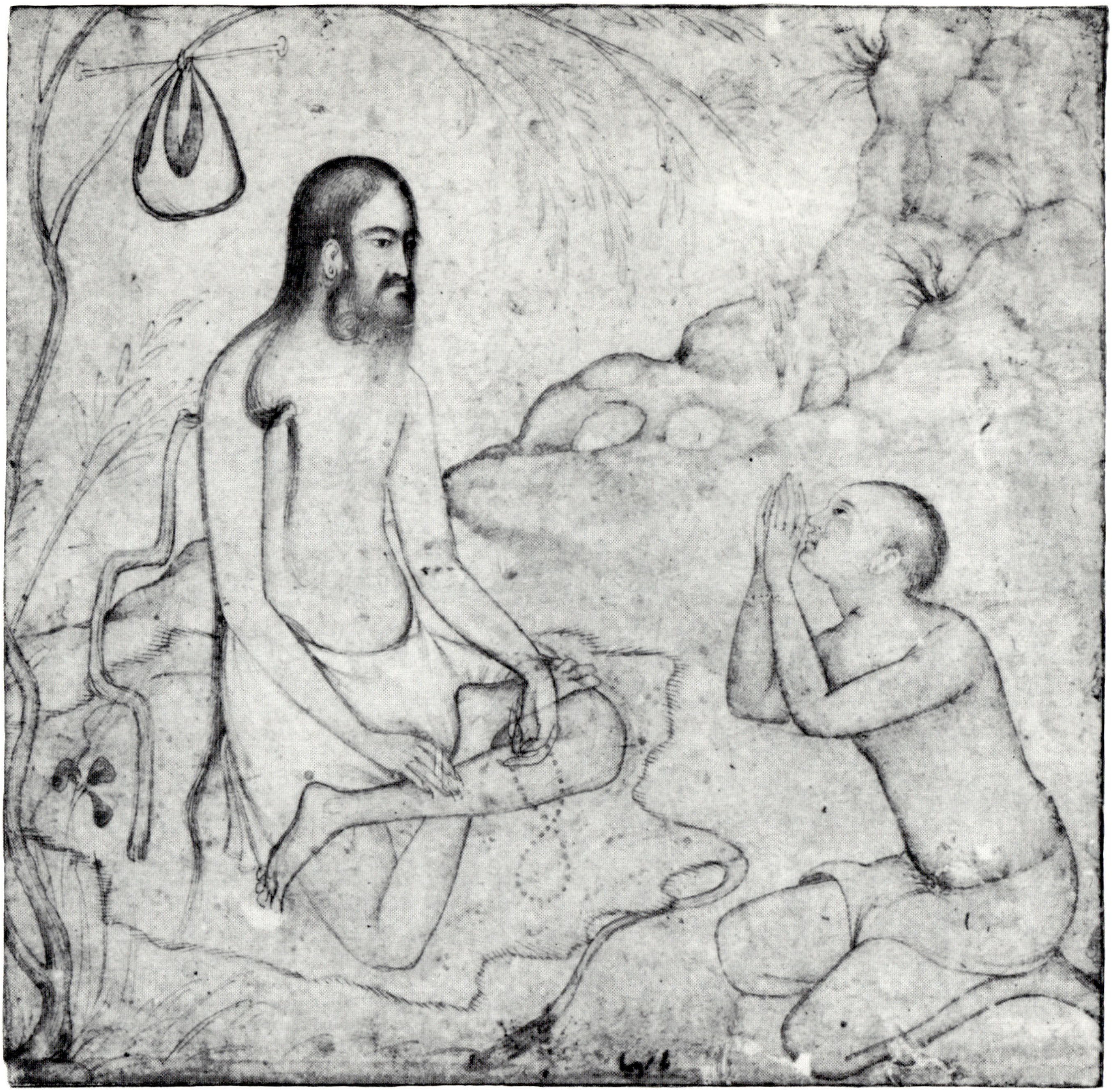

47 **Yogi and disciple**
Mughal, early seventeenth century
Inscribed: *Nanha*
Brush and drawing on paper 70 × 70 mm
Literature: Arts Council, 1982, no. 268
Victoria & Albert Museum IS 229–1951

This exquisitely sensitive drawing which certainly shows some European influence, is probably by the Mughal artist, Nanha, who worked under Akbar and Jahangir, though the inscription on the drawing is not really an attribution. HH

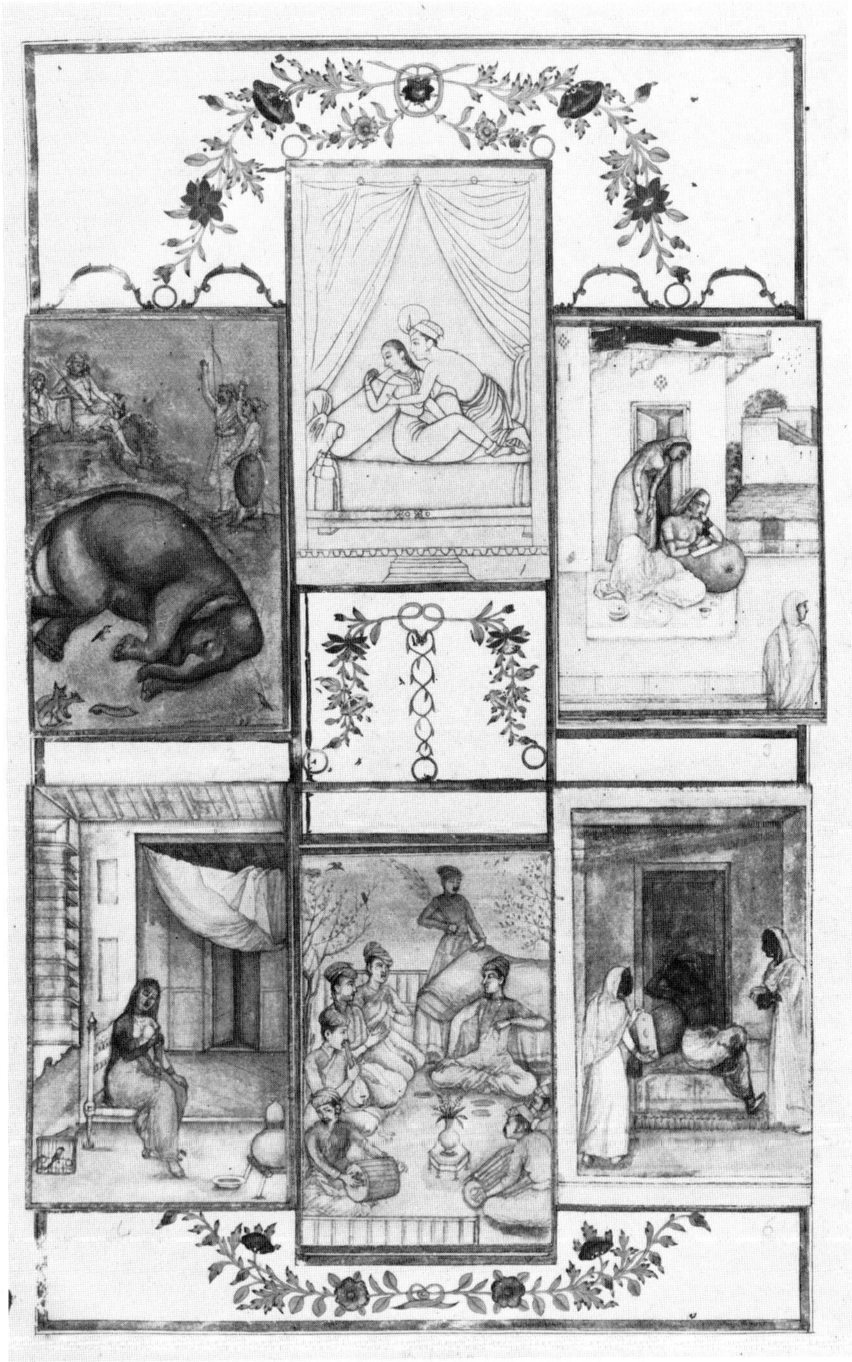

48 i–vi Dipaka Raga and related raginis
Lucknow, *c* 1780–82
Johnson Album 32, no. 1
i **Dipaka Raga** A lord and consort embrace on a bed; a lamp is burning in the lord's turban
Monochrome drawing 114 × 70 mm
ii **Kanada Ragini** Two men salute a warrior near a slain elephant
Drawing with a little colour 113 × 69 mm
iii **Dhanasri Ragini** A lady draws on a tablet with two girls present
Drawing with a little colour 110 × 74 mm
iv **Bairadi Ragini** A lady is seated on a bed holding a garland
Drawing with a little colour 115 × 71 mm
v **Vasanta Ragini** A lord sits listening to six musicians
Drawing with a little colour 108 × 70 mm
vi **Desvarati Ragini** A lady holds her arms above her head and looks into a mirror
Drawing with a little colour 115 × 72 mm
Literature: T. Falk and M. Archer, 1981, p. 164
British Library, India Office Library and Records

A collection of preparatory sketches for paintings of Ragini subjects which are pictorial parallels to, rather than illustrations of, songs about differing states of love.

They are drawings of considerable sensitivity but clearly not all by the same hand. The arrangement on the album page and the rather weak European style garlands connecting the pictures reflect the taste of the European patron for whom the album was assembled. HH

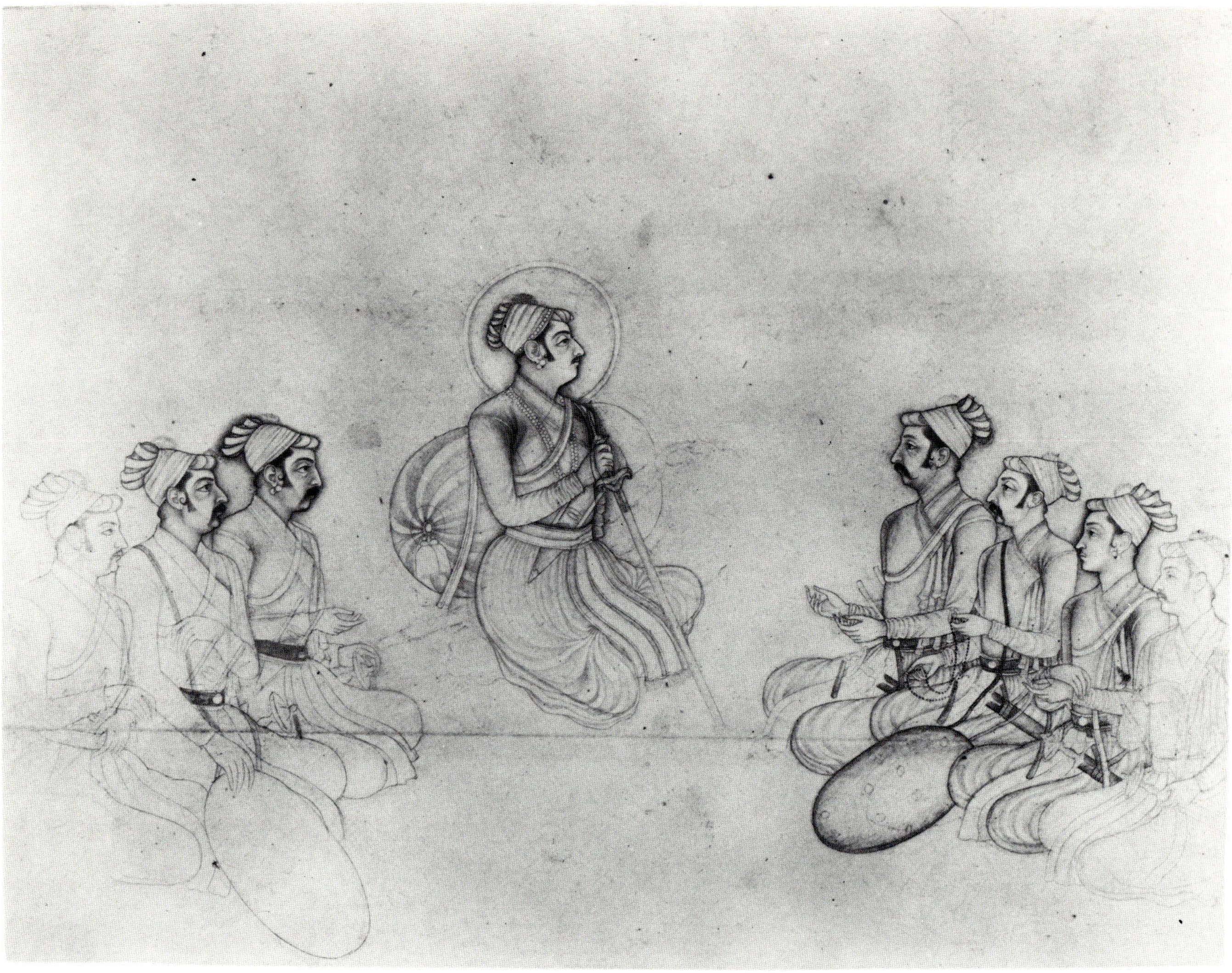

49 **Raja Jaswant Singh of Jodphur giving audience to a group of Rathor Rajputs**
Rajasthan, Jodphur, *c* 1645
Black line with gold and white on paper 160 × 210 mm
Literature: S. C. Welch, 1976, no. 64
Victoria & Albert Museum IS 559–1952 Garey-Anderson Collection

Though made in Rajasthan, this unfinished drawing is essentially Mughal in feeling but its style is already something else. The glacial technique does not disguise the intense humanity of the individual portraits. There are two other drawings by the same hand in the British Museum. HH

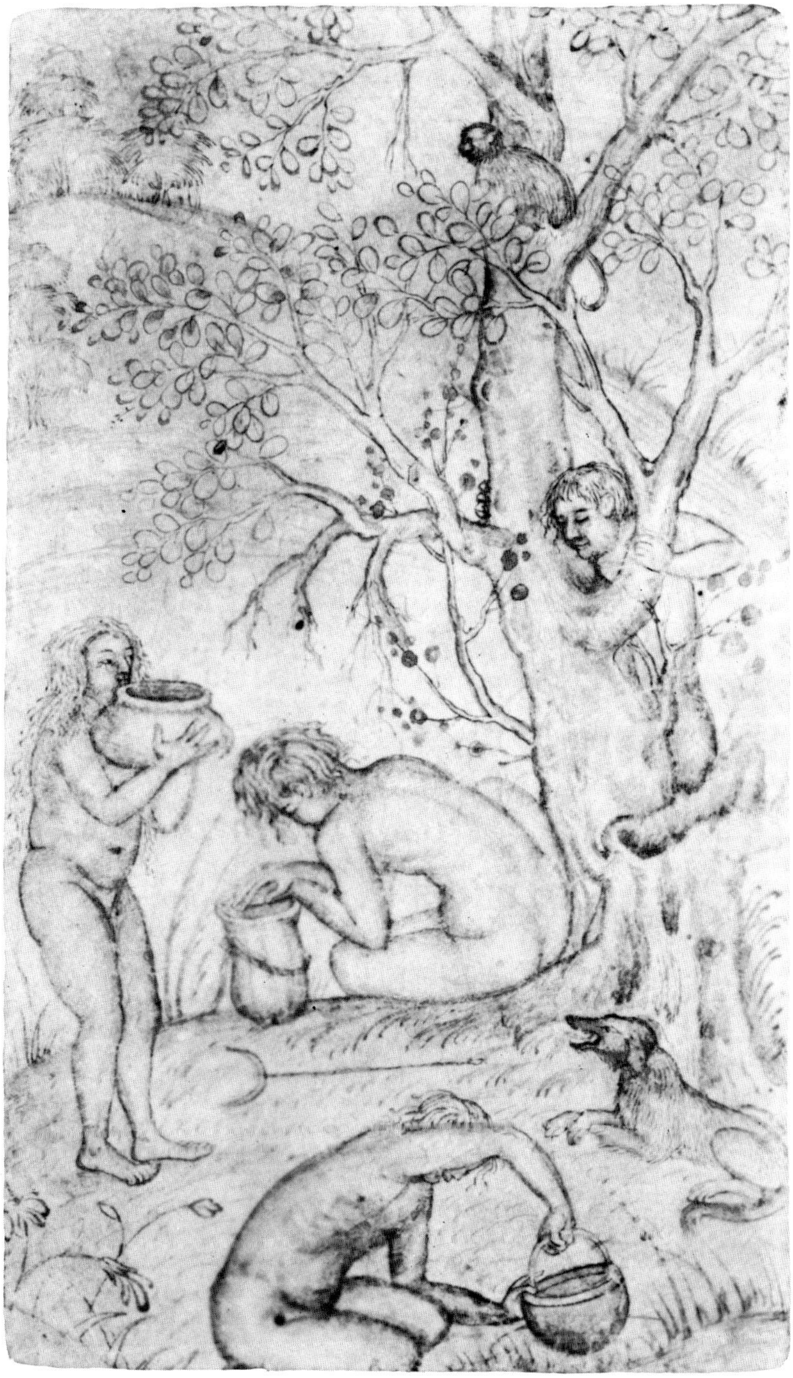

50 **Boys preparing ganja**
Attributed to Basawan, *c* 1620
Mughal, *c* 1620
Point of a brush 139 × 79 mm
Private collection

For another and less formal drawing by the great Basawan, see also *Portrait of an elderly scholar* (no. 1). In this lyrical composition, it is tempting to find traces of European Mannerism, but this is probably misleading. It is quite possible that the eloquent poses of the two central figures are the result of direct observation. HH

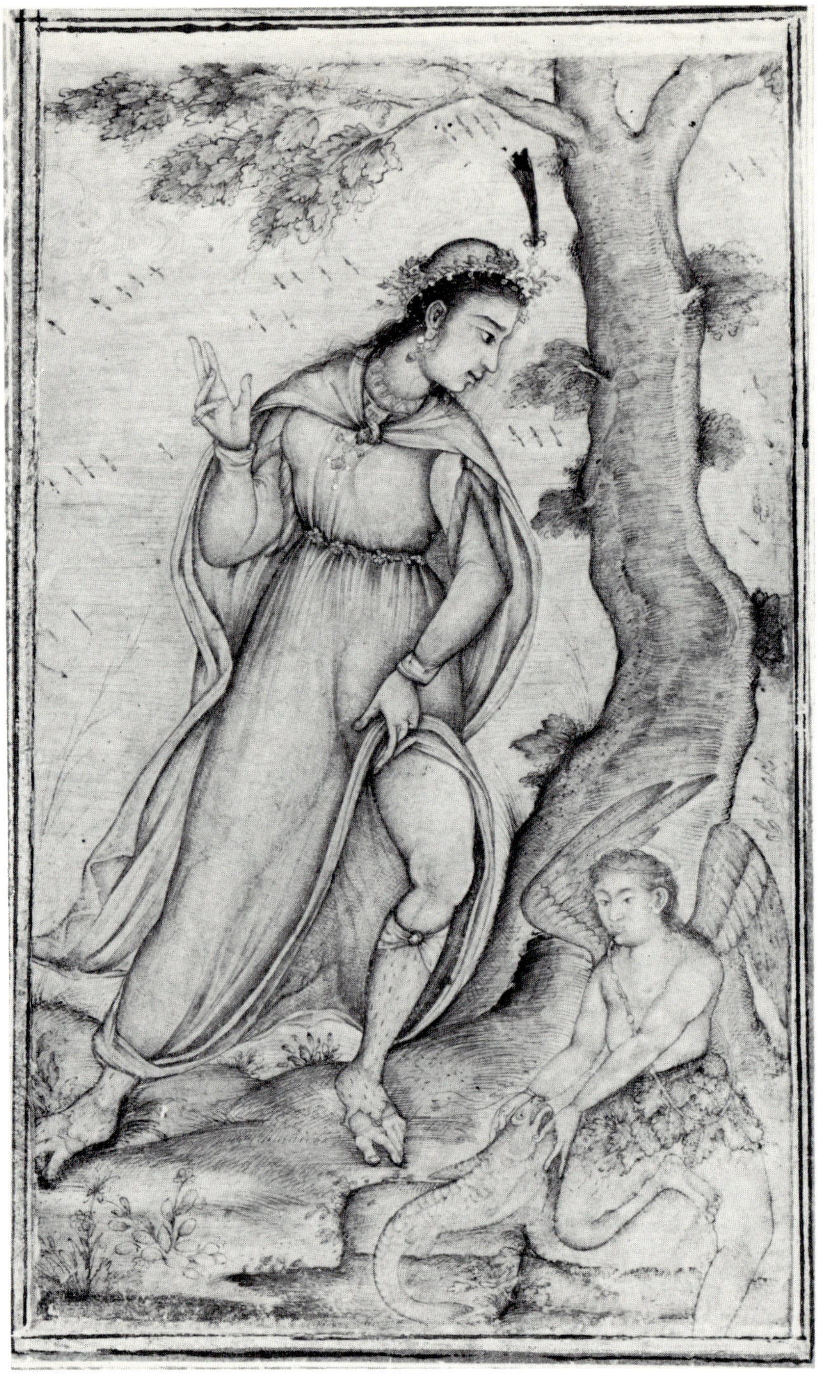

51 Tobias and the Angel
Mughal, *c* 1600
Brush drawing, heightened with gold and colour, on paper
110 × 65 mm
Sven Gahlin

The arrival of engravings, by and after European masters, at the Mughal Court must have been of great pictorial curiosity to Akbar's artists, and many of their paintings and drawings were freely influenced by Biblical (in this case apocryphal) subjects.

The iconography has here become slightly confused in that the young Tobias, in a Bhil's skirt of leaves, is wearing the angel's wings.

HH

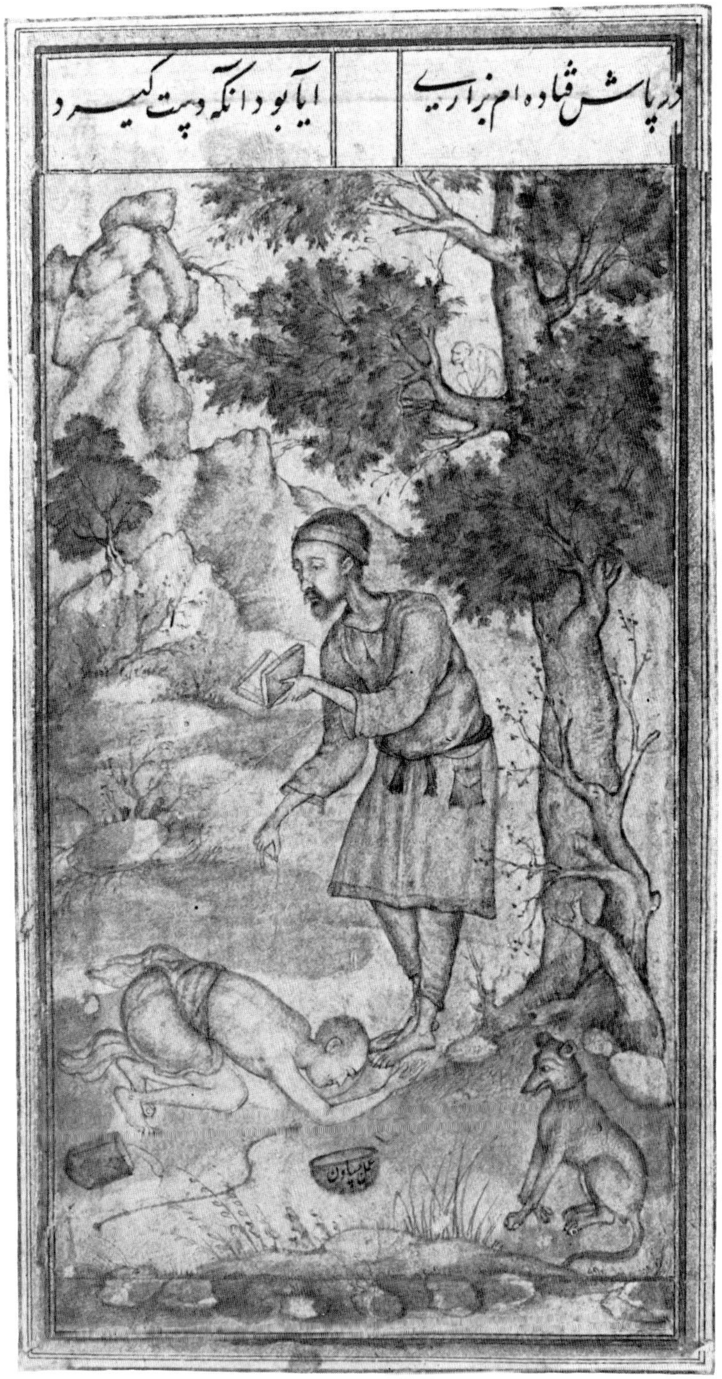

52 An ascetic kneels before a wandering holy man
By Basawan
Mughal, late sixteenth century
Signed on the almsbowl: '*the work of Basawan*'
Drawing in brush and black ink, heightened with tan washes and colour, on paper
Border decorated with geometric figures in gold; mounted on a card 138 × 75 mm; page 327 × 211 mm
From the Prince Khurram Album (now dispersed)
One line of text in *nasta'liq* script
Literature: S. C. Welch, 1961, pp. 7–17
Catherine and Ralph Benkaim Collection

The artist Basawan (fl. 1560–1600) was a pioneer in developing the special category of Mughal drawing – the *nim kalam* – that is represented by the present work. These studies in brush and tan washes have the finish and elaborate detail of fully painted works. Basawan was also famous for his studies of ascetics and holy men of every description. As in the present drawing, the subject is always treated with a remarkable sympathy and gentle humour that gives equal weight to the spiritual as well as the mundane.

For two other works by Basawan, who was perhaps the pre-eminent Indian painter of the sixteenth century, see nos. 1 and 50.

TM

CATALOGUE NOTE

Each catalogue note is followed by the author's initials
HH Howard Hodgkin
TM Terence McInerney

The following bibliographical abbreviations have been used in the catalogue:

Arts Council, 1982
In the Image of Man, exhibition catalogue, Arts Council of Great Britain/Weidenfeld & Nicolson, London 1982

W. G. Archer, 1973
W. G. Archer, *Indian Paintings from the Punjab Hills*, London, 1973

L. Ashton, 1949
L. Ashton (ed) *The Arts of India and Pakistan*, London, 1949

M. C. Beach, 1974
M. C. Beach, *Rajput Painting at Bundi and Kota*, Ascona, 1974

M. C. Beach, 1978
M. C. Beach, *The Grand Mogul: Imperial Painting in India 1600–1660*

P. Brown, 1924
P. Brown, *Indian Painting under the Mughals*, Oxford, 1924

A. K. Coomaraswamy, 1910
A. K. Coomaraswamy, *Indian Drawings*, 2 vols. London, 1910–12

A. K. Coomaraswamy, 1927
A. K. Coomaraswamy, *The History of Indian and Indonesian Art*, New York, 1927

T. Falk & M. Archer, 1981
T. Falk & M. Archer, *Indian Miniatures in the India Office Library*, London 1981

C. A. Glynn, 1979
C. A. Glynn, 'Seven Inscribed Pahari Portraits', *Los Angeles County Museum of Art Bulletin*, Vol XXV, 1979

O. Kurz, 1977
O. Kurz, 'A volume of Mughal Drawings and Miniatures' *The Decorative Arts of Europe and the Islamic East: Selected studies*, London 1977

S. Lee, 1960
S. Lee, *Rajput Painting*, New York, 1960

T. McInerney, 1928
T. McInerney, *Indian Painting 1525–1825*, exhibition catalogue; David Carritt Ltd., London, 1982

H. G. Rawlinson, 1947
H. G. Rawlinson, *Indian Art*, Faber & Faber, London, 1947

P. Rawson, 1972
Philip Rawson, *Indian Art*, Studio Vista/Dutton Picturebook, London and New York, 1972

A. Topsfield, 1980
A. Topsfield, *Painting from Rajasthan in the National Gallery of Victoria*, Melbourne, 1980

S. C. Welch, 1961
S. C. Welch, 'The Paintings of Basawan', *Lalit Kala*, no. 10 1961

S. C. Welch, 1976
S. C. Welch, *Indian Drawings and Painted Sketches*, New York, 1976

J. S. Wilkinson, 1948
J. S. Wilkinson, *Mughal Painting*, London, 1948

ISBN 0 7287 0350 5

Exhibition Organiser: Janet Holt
Exhibition Assistant: Julia Baxter

Photography:
Lending institutions
Prudence Cuming Associates
Bruce Jones/Fine Art Photography, New York
Eileen Tweedy

Catalogue designed by Tim Harvey
Printed in Great Britain by
Balding + Mansell Limited
Cover: detail from **Tiger hunt** (no. 35)